Language Arts Workbook

Siegfried Engelmann

Bernadette Kelly

Karen Davis

Susie Andrist

Jerry Silbert

Acknowledgments

The authors are grateful to the following people for their assistance in the preparations of Reading Mastery Transformations Grade 2 Language.

Amilcar Cifuentes
Gary Davis
Cally Dwyer
Katherine Gries
Debbi Kleppen
Margie Mayo
Patricia McFadden
Melissa Morrow

Trevor Smith
Leta Tillitt
Piper VanNortwick
John Weber
Tina Wells
Nancy Woolfson
Mary Rosenbaum

PHOTO CREDITS

2 (tl)Alan Schein/Alamy Stock Photo, (tc)©Henrik5000/E+/Getty Images, (tr,bl)©Comstock Images/Alamy, (bc)Ljupco/Getty Images, (br)Ingram Publishing/SuperStock; **7** kurhan/123RF; **49** Frank Gaglione/Digital Vision/Getty Images; **52** (tl)Denise McCullough, (tr)Perfect Picture Parts/Alamy, (bl)©Clearviewstock/Alamy, (br)©Leonid Nyshko/Alamy; **56** (tl)William Britten/Getty Images, (tc)Ken Cavanagh/McGraw-Hill Education, (tr)Ken Karp/McGraw-Hill Education, (bl)McGraw-Hill Education, (br)Jill Braaten/McGraw-Hill Education; **59** (tl)Siede Preis/Getty Images, (tc)©Comstock Images/Alamy, (tr)Don Farrall/Getty Images, (bl)Ingram Publishing, (br)©Rene Frederick/Getty Images; **109** (tl)D. Hurst/Alamy Images, (tc)©Photodisc/PunchStock, (tr)Photo Agency EYE/Alamy, (bl)©Ingram Publishing/SuperStock, (br)Author's Image/Glow Images; **113** Blend/Image Source; **115** Purestock/SuperStock; **124** (tl,tc)lynx/iconotec/Glow Images, (tr)Purestock/SuperStock, (bl)©Ingram Publishing/age fotostock, (br)Ingram Publishing/SuperStock; **135** (tl)Ingram Publishing/SuperStock, (tr)Cre8tive Studios/Alamy, (cl)McGraw-Hill Education, (cr)©Comstock Images/Alamy, (bl)©Life on white/Alamy Stock Photo, (br)Mark Dierker/McGraw-Hill Education; **136** McGraw-Hill Education; **137** (tl)©Digital Vision/Getty Images, (tr)USDA Natural Resources Conservation Service, (bl)Peter Turner/Shutterstock.com, (br)Mark Dierker/McGraw-Hill Education; **182** (t,b)George Bernard/Avalon Licensing Limited, (tc)Robert Trevis-Smith/Getty Images, (c)Sebastian Schneider/Getty Images, (bc)Justus de Cuveland/Getty Images; **188** kupicoo/E+/Getty Images; **189** (l)McGraw-Hill Education, (cl)Cre8tive Studios/Alamy Stock Photo, (cr)alexei_tm/Shutterstock, (r)Sean Duan/Moment/Getty Images. **Mastery Tests: T-7** McGraw-Hill Education; **T-9** (tl)AE Pictures Inc./Getty Images, (cl)Aaron Amat/Shutterstock, (cr)belchonock/123RF, (bl)Kichigin/Shutterstock, (br)©gerenme/Getty Images, **T-12** (l)Juniors/SuperStock, (r)Coqrouge/iStock/Getty Images; **T-21** (tl)©Ingram Publishing/SuperStock, (tc)margouillat/123RF, (tr)Kristina Bauer/McGraw-Hill Education, (bl)Christian Jung/Shutterstock, (br)©Ingram Publishing/age fotostock; **T-39** (tl)©Ingram Publishing/Alamy, (tr)McGraw-Hill Education, (bl)ivkuzmin/Getty Images, (br)amstockphoto/Shutterstock.

mheducation.com/prek-12

Copyright © 2021 McGraw-Hill Education

All rights reserved. No part of this publication may be reproduced or distributed in any form or by any means, or stored in a database or retrieval system, without the prior written consent of McGraw-Hill Education, including, but not limited to, network storage or transmission, or broadcast for distance learning.

Permission is granted to reproduce the material contained on pages T-1–T-40 on the condition that such material be reproduced only for classroom use; be provided to students, teachers, or families without charge; and be used solely in conjunction with *Reading Mastery Transformations*.

Send all inquiries to:
McGraw-Hill Education
8787 Orion Place
Columbus, OH 43240

ISBN: 978-0-07-905365-7
MHID: 0-07-905365-3

Printed in the United States of America.

2 3 4 5 6 7 8 SWI 26 25 24 23 22

Name _____

A **Write the words that tell what people did.**

1. burn _____   4. lick _____
2. fill _____   5. start _____
3. push _____   6. scratch _____

B **For each sentence circle reports or does not report.**

1. Ming drove a van to the picnic.   reports   does not report
2. Three people sat at a picnic table.   reports   does not report
3. Everybody was going to swim later that day.   reports   does not report
4. Roberto wore a hat.   reports   does not report
5. Ming ate more than anybody else.   reports   does not report
6. A van was on the grass.   reports   does not report
7. Ming sat next to Mrs. Hudson.   reports   does not report

C Skip a line. Copy each sentence.

1. He ate a green apple.

1.

2. Alice found a dime.

3. David took a walk in the park.

D Write the rest of the conclusion.

- All vehicles can move.
- A car is a vehicle.

So _____

END OF LESSON 1

Name _____

2

A **Copy each sentence just as it is written.**

1. Alex got a nice gift.

1.

2. My sister is ten years old.

3. She fell asleep.

B **Write the words that tell what people did.**

1. jump _____
2. pull _____
3. play _____
4. push _____
5. spill _____
6. trick _____

C **Write the rest of the conclusion.**

- All fish have fins.
- A salmon is a fish.

So _____

Lesson 2

D For each sentence circle reports or does not report.

1. Sherlock ate too much corn.   reports   does not report

2. Bertha was mad at Sherlock.   reports   does not report

3. Cyrus pulled a large sack.   reports   does not report

4. Bertha played a violin.   reports   does not report

5. The wise old rat was dirty.   reports   does not report

6. The sack was full of hazelnuts.   reports   does not report

7. The wise old rat was wet.   reports   does not report

END OF LESSON 2

Name _____

A Copy each sentence just as it is written.

1. The book had more than 200 pages.

2. Her hand hurt for a week.

3. Why did you say that to her?

B Write the words that tell what people did.

1. rest _____
2. walk _____
3. fill _____
4. look _____
5. yell _____
6. test _____

Lesson 3

C For each sentence circle <u>reports</u> or <u>does not report</u>.

1. The three men were brothers. reports does not report

2. Three men fished from a boat. reports does not report

3. The men were going to have fish for dinner. reports does not report

4. A big dog stood in the boat. reports does not report

5. All the men wore hats. reports does not report

6. One man held a net. reports does not report

7. One man was standing up. reports does not report

8. A large fish was on the end of the line. reports does not report

D Write the rest of the conclusion.

- Every worker uses tools.
- A plumber is a worker.

So _____

E Circle the part that names.

1. The old man went to the store.
2. The man and the boy painted a bench.
3. The horse jumped over the fence.
4. An old dog sat in our yard.
5. His brother runs fast.

END OF LESSON 3

4   Name _____

A Write the part that names.

1. _____ stood next to the mother deer.

2. _____ hopped over a log.

3. _____ sat on a log.

B Write the words that tell what people did.

1. find found	6. tell _____	11. dig _____
2. give gave	7. find _____	12. tell _____
3. tell told	8. dig _____	13. have _____
4. dig dug	9. have _____	14. give _____
5. have had	10. give _____	15. find _____

8   Lesson 4

C Complete the item.

- All vehicles can move.
- A _____ is a vehicle.

  So _____ can move.

| truck | boat | train | car | plane | bike |

D Circle the part that names.

1. Two girls are eating ice cream.

2. A black cat ran under the fence.

3. A man and a woman sat on the porch.

4. The old woman lived in a shoe.

5. Dan and his sisters walked home after school.

END OF LESSON 4

5 Name _____

A Write the part that names for each item.

1. _____ held the kite string.

2. _____ climbed the tree.

3. _____ was stuck in the tree.

B Write the words that tell what people did.

1. give gave	6. dig _____	11. find _____
2. dig dug	7. find _____	12. give _____
3. find found	8. tell _____	13. tell _____
4. have had	9. give _____	14. have _____
5. tell told	10. have _____	15. dig _____

C Complete the item.

- Every building has a roof.
- A _____ is a building.

  So _____ has a roof.

| church | house | school | store | shed |

D Circle the part that names.

1. A little girl ate two apples.
2. A cow and a horse ate grass.
3. A kite went high in the sky.
4. My brother washed the dishes.

END OF LESSON 5

6 Name _____

A Complete each sentence.

1. _____	rode a bicycle.
2. _____	juggled three balls.
3. _____	walked on the rope.
4. _____	laughed at the clown.

B Write the words that tell what people did.

1. give _____ 4. have _____
2. dig _____   5. tell _____
3. find _____

C Put the name of the bird you choose in the first blank. Then complete the conclusion.

- Every bird has wings.
- A _____ is a bird.

  So _____ has wings.

turkey   duck   crow   robin   bluebird

D Circle **true** or **false** for each sentence.

1. There were three bragging rats that argued and bragged all the time.   true   false

2. One of the rats had yellow teeth and a very long tail.   true   false

3. The two bragging rats got into a terrible argument about who could run fastest.   true   false

4. The rats argued for days until a little black rat said, "There's a way to find out who is the fastest rat."   true   false

5. The rats had a race down the path to the pond and then back to the starting line.   true   false

6. The rat with yellow teeth stepped on the tail of the gray rat, and both of them went into the pond.   true   false

7. At the end of the story, the bragging rats started a new argument about who could swim the fastest.   true   false

END OF LESSON 6

7 Name _____

A Write the words that tell what people did.

1.	wear	wore
2.	see	saw
3.	run	ran
4.	go	went
5.	sit	sat

6. see _____
7. sit _____
8. go _____
9. wear _____
10. run _____

B Write the name of a tree in the first blank. Then complete the conclusion.

- All trees have leaves.
- A _____ is a tree.

  So _____ has leaves.

maple   fir   cedar   birch   redwood   pine

INDEPENDENT WORK

C Write the word that tells what people did.

1. give _____
2. have _____
3. find _____
4. tell _____
5. dig _____

END OF LESSON 7

Lesson 7

Name _____

A Write the words that tell what people did.

1. see   saw
2. wear   wore
3. sit   sat
4. run   ran
5. go   went

6. wear _____
7. run _____
8. see _____
9. go _____
10. sit _____

B Write the name of the bird in the first blank. Then complete the conclusion.

- Every bird has feathers.
- A _____ is a bird.

   So _____

robin   crow   hawk   chicken   seagull

C Circle the part that names.

1. Five boys ran in the park.

2. His mother and his sister were in the kitchen.

3. The book had more than 400 pages.

4. An old tree stood next to the barn.

INDEPENDENT WORK

D Write the words that tell what people did.

1. dig _____

2. have _____

3. give _____

4. tell _____

5. find _____

END OF LESSON 8

Name _____

A Write the words that tell what people did.

1. see _____
2. go _____
3. sit _____
4. wear _____
5. run _____

B Fill in the blanks with He or She.

1. The girl was running.   _____ was running.
2. My grandfather read a book.   _____ read a book.
3. Katey painted the wall.   _____ painted the wall.
4. Jayden walked home.   _____ walked home.
5. My brother woke up.   _____ woke up.
6. His mother washed her hands.   _____ washed her hands.

C Fix up the sentences so they tell what people did.

1. Alicia was fixing her bike.

2. The girl was talking loudly.

3. Miss Cook was finding her keys.

4. Her grandmother was smiling at the baby.

5. Mr. Howard was telling a story.

D **Circle the part that names. Then underline the part that tells more.**

1. A very young puppy was trying to walk.

2. He laughed at the joke.

3. The oldest girl is Jenny Walker.

4. I like picnics.

5. You can come with us.

E **Complete the deduction.**

In the afternoon, all the toads are on toadstools.

 Where is Jenny the toad in the afternoon?

- In the afternoon, all the toads are _____

- Jenny is _____

- So in the afternoon, Jenny is _____

END OF LESSON 9

Name _____

A **Write the words that tell what people did.**

1. sit _____
2. wear _____
3. run _____
4. see _____
5. go _____

B **Fill in the blanks with He or She.**

1. His sister won the race.   _____ won the race.
2. Her father went to the park.   _____ went to the park.
3. A tall boy washed the car.   _____ washed the car.
4. The young woman fixed the bike.   _____ fixed the bike.

C **Fix up the sentences so they tell what people did.**

1. He is giving her a kiss.
2. Mary and Beth were having fun.
3. We were telling the truth.
4. The man is painting the house.
5. Juan was finding his socks.
6. Miss Clark is digging in the garden.

D **Circle the part that names. Then underline the part that tells more.**

1. You should try harder.

2. Jimmy rode a bike when he was three.

3. She stopped.

4. He can't stop laughing.

5. The book with a brown cover costs a lot of money.

6. That clock doesn't tell time.

E **Complete the conclusion.**

- All old cars make noise.

- A Crumper is an old car.

    So _____

END OF LESSON 10

Name _____

A **Circle the part that names. Then underline the part that tells more.**

1. Her dress is white and red.
2. Our dad works at night.
3. I love popcorn.
4. Mr. Brown's dog barks.
5. You should know better.
6. Our roof leaks.
7. We did well on the test.

B **Write the words that tell what happened.**

1. Maria always hides from me. — Maria always _____ from me.
2. The bird flies away. — The bird _____ away.
3. Dan rides horses well. — Dan _____ horses well.
4. Amy gets sick. — Amy _____ sick.
5. Andy stands alone. — Andy _____ alone.

C **Fill in the blanks with He or She or It.**

1. That coat was covered with dirt. — _____ was covered with dirt.
2. The rubber ball fell off the table. — _____ fell off the table.
3. My father sat in a chair. — _____ sat in a chair.
4. This book was very funny. — _____ was very funny.

Lesson 11

5. The young woman rode a bike.   _____ rode a bike.

6. Susan's game ended early.   _____ ended early.

D Fix up the sentences so they tell what people did.

1. Two children <u>are washing</u> the car.

2. He <u>is spelling</u> a hard word.

3. Elsa <u>is having</u> a party.

4. Nick <u>is telling</u> us what to do.

5. He <u>is finding</u> a pencil.

6. She <u>was filling</u> the glass with water.

INDEPENDENT WORK

E Complete the deduction.

- All vehicles can move.
- A car is a vehicle.

So _____

F Write the words that tell what people did.

1. give _____
2. go _____
3. wear _____
4. run _____
5. dig _____
6. sit _____
7. see _____
8. find _____
9. have _____

END OF LESSON 11

A Circle the part of each sentence that names.

Tina and Sara wanted to play in the water.

The girls were wearing jeans. They went to the little pool. The two girls went into the shallow water. They started to splash each other.

Tina and Sara were all wet when they left the pool.

B Write the words that tell what happened.

1. The soldier stands tall.   The soldier _____ tall.
2. She gets seasick.   She _____ seasick.
3. The mouse hides behind the door. The mouse _____ behind the door.
4. The plane flies fast.   The plane _____ fast.
5. Tom rides his bike to school.   Tom _____ his bike to school.

Lesson 12

C Fill in the blanks with **He**, **She**, or **It**.

1. His big sister parked the car. _____ parked the car.
2. Ted's car slid down the hill. _____ slid down the hill.
3. That movie was interesting. _____ was interesting.
4. Amanda's brother won the race. _____ won the race.
5. The party was fun. _____ was fun.

D Fix up the sentences so they tell what people did.

1. He was having fun.
2. She is looking at the sky.
3. Mia was picking apples.
4. She is telling a funny joke.
5. Ann is digging in the sand.
6. She was folding the paper.

END OF LESSON 12

Name _____

A Write the words that tell what happened.

1. The vase stands on the table. The vase _____ on the table.

2. The dog hides the ball. The dog _____ the ball.

3. Ray flies a kite. Ray _____ a kite.

4. Jill rides the bus every day. Jill _____ the bus every day.

5. The car gets dirty quickly. The car _____ dirty quickly.

B Circle the part of each sentence that names.

	Carla and her friends went to the park.
	Carla played on the swings. She went down
	a slide many times. A very tired Carla rested
	on a bench. Carla and her friends walked home.

Lesson 13

C Fill in the blanks with **He, She,** or **It.**

1. His shirt was covered with dirt. _____ was covered with dirt.

2. My new pencil fell off the table. _____ fell off the table.

3. The girl's father sat in a chair. _____ sat in a chair.

4. Tamika's book was very funny. _____ was very funny.

5. A young woman rode a bike. _____ rode a bike.

D Fix up the sentences so they tell what people did.

1. Vanessa is giving the cup to him.

2. Carlos was jumping over the fence.

3. Four children were finding books in the library.

4. Mr. Lopez was painting a chair.

END OF LESSON 13

Name _____

14

A **Fix up the sentences so they tell what happened.**

1. Tyrell gets a new dog.

2. John hidded the money in his desk.

3. The plane flied over the mountain.

4. Vanessa standed on the table.

5. We seen a clown at the circus.

B **Circle the part of each sentence that names.**

An old cowboy rode his horse to town.

That cowboy wanted to buy a new hat.

He rode his horse to the clothing store.

He tied his horse to a post. The cowboy went into the store. He found a hat he liked.

His horse just loves wearing that hat.

Lesson 14

C Fill in the blanks with He, She, or It.

1. That red plate was broken.   _____ was broken.

2. Her brother fell down.   _____ fell down.

3. My sister had a cold.   _____ had a cold.

4. My father's hat was dirty.   _____ was dirty.

5. An airplane flew over the clouds.   _____ flew over the clouds.

6. Her window was open.   _____ was open.

D Fix up the sentences so they tell what people did.

1. Miss Ross is digging holes for the fence posts.

2. They are filling the box with sand.

3. My grandfather was starting his car.

4. She was having a party.

5. Justin is giving me a ride.

6. The children were cooking eggs.

INDEPENDENT WORK

E **Complete the deduction.**

- All fish can swim.
- A trout is a fish.

So _____

F **Write the words that tell what people did.**

1. sit _____
2. run _____
3. have _____
4. see _____

5. dig _____
6. wear _____
7. give _____
8. go _____

END OF LESSON 14

15 Name _____

A Fix up the sentences so they tell what people did.

1. Lee rided a new bike.

2. We telled about it.

3. He standed on the corner.

4. Carlos getted new gloves for his birthday.

5. My mom sitted next to me.

B Circle the part of each sentence that names.

	A little boy found a small box in his yard.
	The box had three beans in it. The little boy
	showed the beans to his sister. She told him
	to plant the beans. Three plants grew from
	the beans. Those plants were made of gold.

C Fill in the blanks with He, She, or It.

1. Robert spent all morning cleaning his room. _____ put his dirty clothes in the laundry basket.

2. My sister went to the park. _____ played basketball for two hours.

3. The boat held four people. _____ had three sails.

D Fix up the sentences so they tell what people did.

1. They were going to the store.

2. He is filling the sink with hot water.

3. My grandmother was fixing her car.

4. She is having fun.

5. Sophia was wearing a new shirt.

6. A boy is spelling a hard word.

INDEPENDENT WORK

E Write the words that tell what people did.

1. see _____
2. give _____
3. sit _____
4. have _____
5. run _____
6. dig _____
7. go _____
8. find _____
9. wear _____
10. tell _____

END OF LESSON 15

A. Circle the part of each sentence that names.

Alex taught his pet monkey to do many tricks. The monkey even learned how to ride a bicycle. Alex dressed his monkey in a costume one day. Alex and his monkey went to the circus. They showed a clown their tricks. The clown gave the monkey a job in the circus.

B. Fix up the sentences so they tell what happened.

1. The airplane flied for 8 hours.

2. They rided a horse.

3. I seen my brother in the park.

4. Tom hided behind the couch.

5. We standed right next to the water.

C **Fill in the blanks with He or She or It.**

1. His mother liked to fix cars. _____ worked in a car shop.

2. My father stayed home this morning. _____ read a book.

3. The bus stopped. _____ ran out of gas.

D **Fix up any sentence that does not tell what somebody did.**

1. Maria wanted a birthday party.

2. She asked some boys and girls to the party.

3. The boys and girls were giving her some presents.

4. Everybody was having fun.

5. The children were playing games outside.

6. They ate cake and ice cream.

INDEPENDENT WORK

E **Complete the deduction.**

- All animals need water.

- A cat is an animal.

  So _____

END OF LESSON 16

17 Name _____

A **Fill in the blanks with He or She or It.**

1. Jill went ice-skating. _____ skated with her friends on the pond.

2. The motorcycle went by us quickly. _____ made a lot of noise.

3. Her dad slept on the couch. _____ snored loudly.

4. My kite was new. _____ landed in a tree.

B **Fix up any sentence that does not tell what somebody did.**

1. They were having fun at the party.

2. Jessica is wearing a new dress.

3. My brother painted his room.

4. Tom and Al are going home.

5. She parked the car.

6. They were starting to run.

C Fix up three words so they start with m or n.

INDEPENDENT WORK

D Fix the wrong word in each sentence.

1. Today Helen weared her best party dress.

2. My dad digged a hole in our yard.

3. Everybody seen him do it.

4. We always telled the truth.

5. Last week I flied on an airplane.

6. I hided my pen in my pocket.

END OF LESSON 17

18

A **Fill in the blanks with He or She or It.**

1. Jeff spent two hours doing his homework. _____ worked hard.

2. Jane went to the park. _____ sat and watched ducks.

3. The cake tasted great. _____ had whipped cream on top.

4. Fran's mother was tall. _____ was as tall as Fran's dad.

B **Fix up any sentence that does not tell what somebody did.**

Mark looked for a hidden treasure. He is going into his backyard with a shovel. He was digging for a long time. His shovel hit something hard. Mark was reaching into the hole. He pulled something out. He was finding a bone.

Check DID: Does each sentence tell what a person or thing did? (4)

END OF LESSON 18

A Circle the subject of each sentence.

1. Three older boys went to the store.
2. A horse and a dog went to a stream.
3. A man sat on a log.
4. They sat on a bench.
5. My friend and his mother were hungry.
6. My hands and my face got dirty.

B Fix up any sentence that does not tell what somebody did.

Mr. Walters was planting an apple tree. He dug a hole in his yard. He placed the tree in the hole. He is filling the hole with dirt. He is watering the tree. He took good care of the tree.

Check DID: Does each sentence tell what Mr. Walters did? (3)

C Write the correct word above each word that is wrong.

INDEPENDENT WORK

D Write the words that tell what people did.

1. sit _____
2. see _____
3. find _____
4. run _____
5. tell _____
6. wear _____
7. dig _____
8. give _____
9. go _____

E Fix each sentence so it tells what happened.

1. When he gived me the prize I was happy.

2. Sue and Jim rided to the park.

3. We go there last year.

4. My best friends have lots of candy.

5. The teams standed side by side.

6. Bill ranned so fast he won the race.

END OF LESSON 19

20

A **Circle the subject of each sentence.**

1. A jet made a lot of noise.

2. A man and his dog went walking.

3. He ate lunch in the office.

4. My brother and his friends played in the park.

5. A little cat drank milk.

B **Fix up four sentences in the paragraph.**

Mr. Smith and his son are going to the circus.

They looked at lions and tigers. A lion tamer

had a whip in his hand. His whip is making

a loud noise. One lion is jumping through a hoop.

Mr. Smith and his son are having a good time.

Check DID: Does each sentence tell what someone or something did? (4)

INDEPENDENT WORK

C Complete the deduction.

- All kittens drink milk.
- Fluffy is a kitten.

So _____

D Fix the wrong word in each sentence.

1. My family already seen that movie.

2. I never finded my lost purse.

3. The birds all sitted in a row.

4. The fish hided behind the plant.

5. Our dad telled us a story every night.

6. We all gotten lost in the woods.

E Circle the subject of each sentence.

Wendy found a dirty old bicycle at the dump.

She showed it to her brother. He told his sister that the bicycle was in very poor shape. Wendy worked on the bike every day for a month.

It looked like a brand new bike when she was done. She gave it to her brother for his birthday.

Wendy and her brother were very happy.

END OF LESSON 20

A Fix up the paragraph with capitals and periods.

A red kite floated into the sky the wind blew the kite three brown ducks flew near the kite the kite went behind some clouds it went so high that nobody could see it

B Circle the sentence that tells the main thing the group did.

The cats had long tails.

A cat chewed on a string.

The cats played with string.

The string was on the floor.

The woman cut the grass.

The family was outside.

Everybody wore a hat.

The family worked in the yard.

Three men wore coats and hats.

Three men walked through the snow.

The snow was cold.

The men wore snow shoes.

C **Circle the subject of each sentence.**

1. Three older boys went to the store.

2. A horse and a dog went to a stream.

3. A man sat on a log.

4. They sat on a bench.

5. My friend and his mother were hungry.

6. My hands and my face got dirty.

INDEPENDENT WORK

D **Write the words that tell what people did.**

1. go _____   4. see _____   7. give _____

2. sit _____   5. wear _____   8. fly _____

3. run _____   6. find _____   9. stand _____

END OF LESSON 21

A Fix up the paragraph with capitals and periods.

(a woman) rode on a sled (four dogs) pulled the sled (it) went through the deep snow (the woman) was very cold (her dogs) liked the snow (they) slept in the snow

B Circle the sentence that tells the main thing the group did.

A boy swept the floor.

The room was dirty.

The children cleaned the room.

The children were standing.

All the farmers wore coats.

The farmers fed the animals.

All the farmers were in the barn.

The animals were hungry.

Four girls sat in chairs.

The girls had plates and glasses.

Four girls ate a meal.

The girls sat around the table.

C **Circle the subject of each sentence.**

1. My best friend and my sister helped me.
2. She had two dollars.
3. My little sister was sick.
4. The tree fell over.
5. He saw a big bird next to the house.
6. A dog and a cat slept with James.

INDEPENDENT WORK

D **Complete the deduction.**

- All insects have six legs.
- An ant is an insect.

So _____

END OF LESSON 22

A Circle the subject of each sentence. Put in capital letters and periods.

Tom and his brother went shopping for food they bought four apples and six oranges the food cost less than five dollars Tom gave the clerk five dollars the clerk gave Tom change

B Circle the sentence that tells the main thing a group did.

Three cowboys felt tired.   The animals wore clothing.
Two cowboys smiled.   The animals did tricks.
The cowboys looked at the fire.   The animals were inside.
Three cowboys cooked supper.   The animals got food for doing well.

C Complete the deduction.

- All detectives have a magnifying glass.
- Sherlock

- _____
- _____

A Circle the subject of each sentence. Put in capital letters and periods.

Sandy and her dog went for a walk they went to the park a cat ran in front of them the dog started to chase the cat the cat ran up a tree

END OF LESSON 24

A Fill in the blanks with He or She or It.

1. My grandmother loves to walk. _____ walks five miles every day.

2. Her brother is ten years old. _____ is in the fifth grade.

3. Our plane will leave at four o'clock. _____ is going to China.

B Circle the subject of each sentence. Put in capital letters and periods.

A woman bought a new bike for her son it had big tires the boy liked the bike his mother showed him how to ride the bike he rode it to school his teacher let him show the bike to the class

END OF LESSON 25

Name _____

26

A Circle the subject of each sentence. Put in capital letters and periods.

Three workers built a doghouse a woman nailed boards together she used a big hammer a young man put a roof on the doghouse the workers finished the doghouse in two hours

B COMPOUND WORDS

1. treetop   2. sandbox   3. doorknob   4. hilltop

C Change the subject in some sentences to **He**, **She**, or **It**.

ᵃSusan loved birds. ᵇSusan wanted to build a birdhouse.

ᶜHer grandfather gave Susan a book about birdhouses.

ᵈHer grandfather told Susan to read it carefully. ᵉThe book was interesting. ᶠThe book showed how to build a birdhouse.

END OF LESSON 26

27

A Put in the missing capital letters and periods.

every student in the class read a book. Tom and Alice read a book about animals they learned about animals that live in different parts of the world. Two students read a book about roses that book told how to take care of roses.

B Complete each item.

1. house

Fran_____

2. tree

Bob_____

3. TV

Turner_____

4. coat

Sally_____

C **Begin each part of a person's name with a capital letter.**

1. mrs. davis
2. the doctor
3. his brother
4. bob washington
5. jerry radley
6. this boy
7. mr. garcia
8. the girl
9. my nurse
10. mrs. cash

D **Change the subject in some sentences to He, She, or It.**

 ᵃThe class was playing football during recess. ᵇTom had the football. ᶜTom threw the ball as far as he could. ᵈAlice jumped up and caught the ball. ᵉAlice scored a touchdown. ᶠThe school bell rang. ᵍThe school bell told the class that recess was over.

END OF LESSON 27

28

A Put in the missing capital letters and periods.

My class had a picnic everybody went on a bus. Our teacher brought apples and oranges. He also cooked a chicken we built a fire to cook the chicken

B Complete each item.

1. the bones that belong to the dog

   the dog's bones

2. the car that belongs to his friend

   his friend_____

3. the arm that belongs to the girl

   the girl_____

4. the books that belong to my sister

   my sister_____

5. the tail that belongs to the cat

   the cat_____

6. the house that belongs to Ray

   Ray_____

C Start each name with a capital letter.

1. They went to my brother's house.
2. mr. and mrs. collins have a new car.
3. Two brothers took their dog, fido, to the lake.
4. They climbed a large oak tree.
5. They heard toads and frogs croaking.
6. I don't agree with henry or his father.

D Change the subject in some of the sentences to He, She, or It.

^aJohn wanted to have a party for his birthday. ^bJohn was going to be ten years old. ^cHis mother planned a big party. ^dHis mother called all of John's friends. ^eHis mother bought lots of party things. ^fThe party started right after school. ^gThe party was a lot of fun.

END OF LESSON 28

A. Put in the missing capital letters and periods.

A little bird fell out of a tree Bill and his sister saw the little bird. it was in a pile of leaves Bill picked up the little bird his sister climbed up to the nest Bill handed the bird to his sister she put the bird back in the nest.

B. Write the compound word for each picture.

tooth   light   door   sail   shoe
lace   boat   house brush knob

1.
_____

2.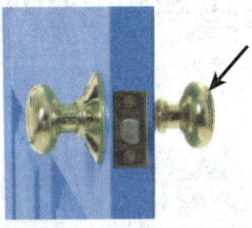
_____

3.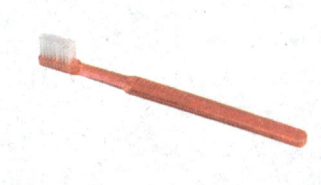
_____

4.
_____

5.
_____

C Write a sentence that tells about all the pictures. Then complete each item.

1.
2.
3.

_____

| white | black | big | small |

1. A _____ cat sat on a _____ chair.
2. A _____ cat sat on a _____ chair.
3. A _____ cat sat on a _____ chair.

D Fix up any sentence that should use He, She, or It.

Greg's room was a mess. Greg's room had toys all over the floor. Greg cleaned up his room. Greg put all his clothes in the closet. His grandmother was very happy. His grandmother gave him a big hug.

END OF LESSON 29

A Put in the missing capital letters and periods.

Tom threw a rock at a tree his rock hit a beehive. the bees got very mad they flew out of the nest. Tom ran away from the bees. many bees chased him tom jumped into the lake. he never threw rocks at trees again

B Rewrite the underlined part of each item so it has a word with an apostrophe.

1. Harry found a ball that belongs to his dog.

    Harry found _____.

2. The shirt that belongs to the boy was red.

    _____ was red.

3. We like the mittens that belong to the baby.

    We like _____.

4. The ring that belongs to Henry costs a lot of money.

    _____ costs a lot of money.

5. The head that belongs to my dad has no hair.

   _____ has no hair.

6. We rode in a <u>car that belongs to her sister</u>.

   We rode in her _____ .

C Write the compound word for each picture.

| bed | gold | water | back | basket |
| ball | fall | pack | room | fish |

1.
   _____

2.
   _____

3.
   _____

4.
   _____

5.
   _____

D Write a sentence that tells about all the pictures. Then complete each item.

1.
2.
3.

_____

| young | beach | tennis | old |

1. An _____ woman held a _____ ball.

2. A _____ woman held a _____ ball.

3. An _____ woman held a _____ ball.

E **Fix up any sentence that should use He, She, or It.**

Sandra wanted to play baseball. Sandra looked for her ball and bat. Her brother also wanted to play baseball. Her brother helped her look for the ball and bat. Sandra looked in the yard. Sandra found the ball and bat near the doghouse. The ball was in bad shape. The ball was all chewed up.

END OF LESSON 30

31 Name

A Put in the missing capital letters and periods.

Snow fell all night long. Doris got up and looked outside everything was white. Doris thought about things to do in the snow she wanted to throw snowballs. She wanted to roll in the snow. her mother handed her a snow shovel. Doris went out in the snow She did not have a lot of fun

B Rewrite each underlined part so it has a word with an apostrophe.

1. The hat that belongs to the cat is under the table.

   _____ is under the table.

2. She found coins that belong to her brother.

   She found _____ .

3. They sold books that belong to their grandmother.

   They sold _____ .

4. The TV that belongs to Ann is on all the time.

   _____ is on all the time.

5. The bike that belongs to Alex is missing.

   _____ is missing.

Lesson 31

C Fill in the blanks with **He**, **She**, **It**, or **They**.

1. A man and woman ate dinner. _____ liked the food a lot.
2. Two boys walked on the sand. _____ also went surfing.
3. Our bus had a flat tire. _____ ran over a nail.
4. Bananas cost 68 cents. _____ cost less than apples.
5. The men wore red jackets. _____ were talking to each other.
6. My Uncle Henry ran fast. _____ had to catch the bus.

INDEPENDENT WORK

D Write the words that tell what people did.

1. go _____
2. sit _____
3. run _____
4. find _____
5. wear _____
6. fly _____
7. see _____
8. give _____

END OF LESSON 31

32

A. Put in the missing capital letters and periods.

a strong wind blew down a tree and a fence a boy and a girl saw the broken fence the boy got a can of paint the girl got a hammer and nails they worked very hard to fix the fence

B. Put in the missing apostrophes.

1. six chairs
2. my fathers chairs
3. my fathers chair
4. some apples
5. that trees leaves
6. a cars headlights
7. a boys kites
8. two big oranges
9. those red cars
10. that persons books
11. the teachers pencil
12. the tallest girls

C. Put in the missing capital letters.

1. ruth garcia
2. a doctor
3. a big building
4. fairview hospital
5. don's supermarket
6. dr. ray brown
7. that avenue
8. salt lake city
9. mr. jordan
10. his street
11. florida
12. spring avenue

Lesson 32

D Fill in the blanks with He, She, It, or They.

1. A cow and a horse slept in the barn. _____ stayed warm all night.

2. My shoes were wet. _____ got wet in the rain.

3. Anna played baseball. _____ was the best hitter on her team.

4. A boy shouted. _____ needed our help.

5. His sister stood in line. _____ was buying tickets.

6. A bottle fell off the table. _____ broke on the floor.

7. Bill and Sue went fishing. _____ made fish stew for dinner.

INDEPENDENT WORK

E Rewrite each underlined part so it has a word with an apostrophe.

1. The shirt that belongs to the boy was red.

   _____ was red.

2. The friend that belongs to Mary is very tall.

   _____ is very tall.

3. I like to read the books that belong to my sister.

   I like to read _____ .

END OF LESSON 32

Lesson 32   65

33

A Put in the missing capital letters and periods.

A dog ran after a cat. The animals ran through the kitchen and the living room. They ran up the stairs and down the stairs. The dog ran slower and slower. The cat kept going faster. The dog stopped and sat down. The cat was not even tired.

B Put in the missing apostrophes.

1. a girl's hairbrush
2. that cat's tail
3. the birds in the tree
4. the bugs on the table
5. an old man's face
6. those cats near John
7. the woman's umbrella
8. many cups
9. a boy's suitcases

C Put in the missing capital letters.

1. We went to the zoo on tuesday.

2. In january, we got a new dog.

3. The airport in chicago was busy during may.

4. We went to the park for robert's birthday party.

5. The carlton zoo has more than ten elephants.

6. They liked mr. wood's paintings.

D Fill in the blanks with He, She, It, or They.

1. Two women fixed the car. _____ did it in less than an hour.

2. My father bought a new tie. _____ wore it to the party.

3. The boys and girls played baseball. _____ had a lot of fun.

4. Jill found ten dollars. _____ gave it to her mom.

5. His bag was full of apples. _____ was very heavy.

6. Those apples were not ripe. _____ were too hard to bite.

7. Her sisters fixed Jim's car. _____ did it for free.

8. David fed the dog. _____ liked to take care of his pets.

END OF LESSON 33

34

A Put in the missing capital letters.

1. The holiday thanksgiving is always on thursday.
2. The memorial day holiday is always in may.
3. The 4th of july is also called independence day.
4. I'm going out on halloween with jamal and carlos.
5. I gave a great card to my mother on valentine's day.

B Change the subject in some sentences to He, She, It, or They.

Alex and Sasha went to the airport. Alex and Sasha were going to fly to Dallas. Alex had never been on a plane before. Alex was very frightened. Alex and Sasha sat together on the plane. Alex and Sasha had fun after Alex stopped worrying.

INDEPENDENT WORK

C Rewrite each underlined part. Use an apostrophe.

1. The hand that belonged to her mother was sore.

   _____ was sore.

2. I dented the car that belongs to my dad.

   I dented _____ .

3. He broke the glasses that belonged to Ann.

   He broke _____ .

END OF LESSON 34

Name _____

35

A **Check the paragraph. Fix any mistakes.**

A woman drove an old car she has the car for many years. She took good care of her car. She even was painting the car. Her car looked as good as new everybody likes that wonderful old car.

Check CP: Does each sentence begin with a capital letter and end with a period? **CP** ___

Check DID: Does each sentence tell what somebody did? **DID** ___

B **Write the missing subjects.**

Three women worked on a house. _____ wore work clothes. _____ cut a board. _____ used a saw. _____ carried three pieces of wood. _____ carried the boards on her shoulder. _____ hammered nails into the wood.

Kayla   Bella   Rosa

Lesson 35

C Put in the missing capital letters.

1. we were in new york on new year's day.

2. they went to a labor day party at the sherman hotel.

3. mr. sanchez cooked our turkey for thanksgiving dinner.

4. we will be in stanley park on memorial day.

5. how many cards did you get on valentine's day last monday?

D Write the words the way Bleep would say them.

1. plant _____
2. slam _____
3. clap _____
4. sleep _____

END OF LESSON 35

70 Lesson 35

Name _____

A **Use the checks to fix up the paragraph.**

   A car went past our house. It has old tires it had four broken doors. The car was making lots of noise smoke came out of the hood. The driver is getting out of the car he is kicking the car his car fell apart.

Check CP: Does each sentence begin with a capital letter and end with a period?

CP ___

Check DID: Does each sentence tell what somebody or something did?

DID ___

B **Write the contraction for each word pair.**

1. is not _____
2. would not _____
3. can not _____
4. had not _____

Lesson 36   71

C Write the missing subjects.

Two women were walking. _____ were taking Ben to his room. _____ sat in the wheelchair. _____ wore pajamas. The _____ had big wheels and little wheels. _____ had a seat, a back, and two handles. _____ held a purse. _____ wore a skirt and a sweater. _____ was behind the wheelchair. _____ pushed the wheelchair.

INDEPENDENT WORK

D Put in the missing capital letters.

1. we walk our dog in baker park on sunday mornings.

2. every may we visit my grandma for mother's day.

3. mr. clark went to see wendy on valentine's day.

4. who knows if thanksgiving is on a thursday this year?

E **Rewrite each underlined part so it has a word with an apostrophe.**

1. We tried to fix <u>the tire that belongs to my bike.</u>

    We tried to fix _____ .

2. <u>The nest that belongs to the bird</u> had eggs in it.

    _____ had eggs in it.

3. The fly landed on <u>the head that belongs to a cow.</u>

    The fly landed on _____ .

F **Fix the wrong word in each sentence.**

1. The clown weared big shoes.

2. I rided my bicycle to the park.

3. My uncle given me a book for my birthday.

4. We seen lots of frogs in the pond.

5. The birds flied together in a big flock.

END OF LESSON 36

37

A **Put in the missing capital letters.**

James had two good friends. Their names were jill adams and robert gomez. jill and robert went to the same school that james went to. Their teacher was mr. ray. (9)

Check N: Does each part of a person's name begin with a capital letter?

N ___

B **Write the contraction for each word pair.**

1. there is _____
2. I am _____
3. you are _____
4. should not _____
5. let us _____
6. we are _____
7. here is _____

C Fix up the paragraph.

Morgan threw a flying disc to his dad. And it went over his dad's head. And then his dad ran after the flying disc. And then he tripped in the mud. Morgan started to run after the flying disc. And a big dog picked it up before Morgan could grab it. And then the dog ran away with it. And then Morgan chased after the dog. His dad went in the house to clean up.

D Write the missing subjects.

_____ and _____ worked in the garden. _____ wore hats. _____ dug a hole. _____ pushed the shovel down with her foot. _____ sawed a branch. _____ held the branch with one hand.

END OF LESSON 37

38   Name _____

A Write the contraction for each word pair.

1. are not _____
2. they are _____
3. he is _____
4. I will _____
5. what is _____
6. you will _____
7. where is _____

B Put in the missing capital letters.

1. Henry's lugstuff bag holds a lot of things.
2. We bought a gallon of harvest ripe juice at the market.
3. I don't like yummy honey gum because it is too sweet.
4. Have a cup of sleep easy tea before going to bed.
5. I love my cozy wrap raincoat.

C Fix up the paragraph.

   Sandra went to the zoo yesterday. And then she met her friends near the monkey house. And the monkeys were doing tricks. Two monkeys were swinging by their tails. And one monkey was doing flips. And then Sandra and her friends went to the snack bar. And they bought peanuts for the monkeys.

INDEPENDENT WORK

D **Rewrite each underlined part.**

1. <u>The bottle that belongs to the baby</u> has milk in it.

   _____ has milk in it.

2. We want to buy <u>the bike that belongs to Rob</u>.

   We want to buy _____ .

3. <u>The pencil that belongs to the boy</u> is yellow.

   _____ is yellow.

E **Put in the missing capital letters and periods.**

We had fun after school we went to the pool my friends and I swam and splashed in the water at 5 o'clock, we went home.

END OF LESSON 38

A Put in the missing capital letters.

1. The best-selling brand in our town is soft baked donuts.

2. Look years younger with wrinkle free cream.

3. Buy florence shirts if you want the finest.

4. We're giving children fruity drop candy this Halloween.

5. We learn about the best deals by reading the weekly shopper newspaper.

B Write the contraction for each word pair.

1. we would _____

2. she would _____

3. I am _____

4. can not _____

5. I would _____

6. here is _____

7. you would _____

C Use the checks to fix up the paragraph.

Everybody went to the beach. And Jerry and alice built a fire on the sand. And then Tom and bill roasted hot dogs and marshmallows. And Mr. jones and sammy played ball.

Check AND: Did you fix each sentence that started with **and** or **and then**?

AND ___

Check N: Does each part of a person's name begin with a capital letter?

N ___

INDEPENDENT WORK

D Circle the subject of each sentence.

1. A jet made a lot of noise.
2. A man and his dog went walking.
3. He ate lunch in the office.
4. My brother and his friend played in the park.
5. A little cat drank milk.

END OF LESSON 39

A Write the contraction for each word pair.

1. we would _____
2. is not _____
3. you are _____
4. I would _____
5. she is _____
6. I am _____
7. we are _____
8. could not _____
9. let us _____
10. he would _____

B Fix up each run-on sentence.

1. Two girls played football and their dad watched them and then they asked him if he wanted to play.

2. A boy asked his mother for some food and then she gave him an apple and he asked if he could also have some cheese and his mother gave him a piece of cheese.

C Put in the missing apostrophes.

1. his brothers friends
2. the oldest boys
3. the girls hats
4. Mrs. Longs coat
5. the shortest books
6. my uncles sisters
7. the books cover
8. those houses

INDEPENDENT WORK

D **Capitalize the product name in each sentence.**

1. Will thinks superdunk shoes are the best for basketball.

2. I deliver the lincoln weekly newspaper on Saturdays.

3. We like to buy juicy roll snacks for a treat.

4. Our morning glow cream keeps you looking your best.

E **Capitalize each person's name.**

1. jane cristion
2. her uncle
3. mr. holland
4. that tall woman
5. his brother
6. paul robins
7. helen troy
8. mrs. holmes
9. two sisters

F **Put in the missing capital letters and periods.**

they didn't know what was in the box Joanne picked up the box she said it was very light Robert opened it and looked inside he found out it was empty

END OF LESSON 40

A **Fix up each run-on sentence.**

1. Mr. Clark went for a ride in the country and then his car ran out of gas and then he had to walk three miles to a gas station.

2. Kathy likes to read books and her favorite book was about horses and her brother gave her that book.

3. Emma's mother asked Emma to mow the lawn and then Emma started to cut the grass and she saw that it was too wet.

B **Underline the word pairs. Then write the contractions.**

Sidney and Jade loved to build things. One day, Sidney said, "I would like to build a boat."

Jade said, "That is a difficult thing to do. We would need boards to build it."

Sidney said, "It is easy to get boards. I will buy the things we would need."

Jade said, "I can get the tools. Let us start work next week."

"My brother loves boats," Sidney said. "Maybe he would want to help us build the boat."

END OF LESSON 41

Name _____

A **Put in the missing capital letters and periods.**

We had a good time at the park Tom played basketball with bob. Alice and jane went jogging. I listened to mr. anderson read from a book my sister went swimming we got home just in time for dinner.

Check CP: Does each sentence begin with a capital letter and end with a period? **CP** ___

Check N: Does each part of a person's name begin with a capital letter? **N** ___

B **Underline the word pairs. Then write the contractions.**

Tom wanted a pet dog, but his mother did not like that idea. His mother said, "I do not think we have room for a dog."

"I will take care of the dog," Tom said. "I can take it for walks, and I will train it. Maybe you would like a small dog."

His mother said, "But maybe a small dog would not like me."

Tom said, "We will talk more about this later."

His mother said, "Maybe you will have to talk to yourself."

END OF LESSON 42

43

A Fix up each run-on sentence.

1. Miss Wilson saw a used bike at a store and the bike was red and blue and then Miss Wilson bought it for her sister. (3)

2. Richard and his sister went to a movie and it was very funny and Richard and his sister ate popcorn and then their mother and father picked them up after the movie. (4)

B Underline the word pairs. Then write the contractions.

"Where is my book?" Todd asked. "I can not find it."

"Let me help you," his mom said. "We will both look for the book and find it. Let us look in your room first." So they did.

Todd said, "It is over here!"

His mom said, "And here is our missing pen."

"Thanks, mom," Todd said. "We are a good team."

END OF LESSON 43

Name _____

A. Underline the word pairs. Then write the contractions.

Jan and Bill wanted to teach their dog to sit. Jan said, "I will teach. You will look."

"I do not want to look," Bill said. "I would like to teach."

"You can not teach well," Jan said.

Bill said, "I am good at teaching."

Jan said, "I do not think so. You did not teach a dog before."

Bill said, "When did you ever teach a dog?"

Jan said, "I did not teach any dogs, but I know how to do it."

Just then, their dad came outside and said, "I will teach the dog to sit." So that is what he did.

INDEPENDENT WORK

B. Put in the missing capital letters.

1. the bensons use grow-well plant food in their yard.

2. by december, ruby is done with her christmas shopping.

3. he'll go to richfield hospital this thursday.

4. every saturday, mrs. allen walks from Henley to wilton.

END OF LESSON 44

A **Use the checks to fix up the paragraph.**

Sam and Ellen are cooking supper for their family. Ellen made hamburgers she cooked them over a fire. Sam makes corn he was putting butter and salt on each piece. Everyone likes the meal.

Check CP: Does each sentence begin with a capital letter and end with a period?

Check DID: Does each sentence tell what somebody or something did?

B **Group Leader: Write the number of students who vote for each story.**

How many students?

1. The Bragging Rats Have a Race   ___

2. The Mouse and the Toadstool   ___

3. Goober's Farm   ___

4. The Case of the Missing Corn   ___

5. Bleep the Robot   ___

INDEPENDENT WORK

C **Write the contraction below each word pair.**

1. is not
   _____
2. I am
   _____
3. what is
   _____

4. I will
   _____
5. she would
   _____
6. did not
   _____

D **Put in the missing capital letters.**

1. we eat tasty tots for lunch on mondays.

2. ron likes to run around rowland park to stay fit.

3. when ann comes home we make choco-bake cookies.

4. the sun shines more in may than in april.

END OF LESSON 45

A **Fix up each sentence to show what Bleep would say.**

1. This lamp goes in the bag.
2. I ran on the track.
3. The stamps are in a stack.

INDEPENDENT WORK

B **Write the contraction for each word pair.**

1. you are _____
2. I would _____
3. can not _____
4. that is _____
5. let us _____
6. are not _____

END OF LESSON 46

Name _____

A **Circle the words that tell about more than one thing.**

1. cat 2. cow 3. books 4. brush 5. shoes

6. door 7. beds 8. hat 9. card 10. rags

B

END OF LESSON 48

49   Name _____

A   Circle the correct meaning of each word.

1. reread
   - the opposite of read
   - read again

2. uncover
   - the opposite of cover
   - cover again

3. unclean
   - the opposite of clean
   - clean again

4. replay
   - the opposite of play
   - play again

5. unlock
   - the opposite of lock
   - lock again

B   Add s or es to tell about more than one.

1. rag
2. wish
3. class
4. track
5. fire
6. itch
7. pass
8. bench
9. book
10. brush
11. song

INDEPENDENT WORK

C **Rewrite each underlined part so it has a word with an apostrophe.**

1. The book that belongs to my brother is on the floor.

   _____ is on the floor.

2. The cat sits on the lap that belongs to Jim.

   The cat sits on _____ .

3. The ball that belongs to my dog is missing.

   _____ is missing.

D **Write the contraction for each word pair.**

1. we will _____
2. it is _____
3. they are _____
4. he would _____
5. do not _____
6. where is _____

END OF LESSON 49

50 Name _____

A Use the checks to fix up the paragraph.

	A bluebird sat on a tree branch.
DID	A striped cat was running up the trunk
CP	of the tree to get the bird. The cat ran
	toward the bird The bird flew away. The
M	branch broke. The cat held out its paws.

Check M: Does each sentence tell the main thing?

Check CP: Does each sentence begin with a capital letter and end with a period?

Check DID: Does each sentence tell what something did?

B For each word, write the word that means the opposite.

1. agree

2. appear

_____ _____

3. like

4. honest

_____ _____

C Add s or es to tell about more than one.

1. dash
2. flag
3. coach
4. flash
5. bunch
6. miss
7. mitt
8. bar
9. lash

D Complete the paragraph to give a clear picture.

> He threw a stick into it. The animals jumped into the water and swam after it. They got it and carried it back to him. He used it to dry them before they went home.

_____ threw a stick into

_____ . _____ jumped into

the water and swam after _____ . They got

_____ and carried it back to _____ .

He used _____ to dry _____

before they went home.

Check CP: Does each sentence begin with a capital letter and end with a period?

Check Clear: Does each sentence give a clear picture of what happened?

END OF LESSON 50

Lesson 50

51   Name _____

A **Circle the correct meaning of each word.**

1. remake
   - the opposite of make
   - make again

2. disorder
   - the opposite of order
   - order again

3. reorder
   - the opposite of order
   - order again

4. dislike
   - the opposite of like
   - like again

5. disagree
   - the opposite of agree
   - agree again

6. rethink
   - the opposite of think
   - think again

B **Write the words that tell about more than one thing.**

1. loaf

   _____

2. shelf

   _____

3. wolf

   _____

END OF LESSON 51

Name _____

52

A Write the words that tell about more than one thing.

1. lunch _____
2. loaf _____
3. brush _____
4. sister _____
5. beach _____
6. grass _____
7. wolf _____
8. splash _____
9. bank _____
10. wish _____
11. shelf _____
12. catch _____

B Write dis or un to make words that mean the opposite.

1. _____ kind
2. _____ do
3. _____ agree
4. _____ honest
5. _____ fit
6. _____ obey

Lesson 52   95

C Use the checks to fix the paragraph.

CP	A cowboy fell off a bull. the bull charged
DID	at the cowboy. A clown was putting a
M	barrel in front of the bull. The clown helped
	the cowboy walk away from the bull.

Check M: Does each sentence tell the main thing?

Check CP: Does each sentence begin with a capital letter and end with a period?

Check DID: Does each sentence tell what somebody or something did?

END OF LESSON 52

96 Lesson 52

Name _____

53

A Complete each sentence.

> myself   yourself   himself   herself   itself

1. She sat in the room by _____ .

2. I sang to _____ in the back yard.

3. It saw _____ in the mirror.

4. He ran home by _____ .

5. You did that by _____ .

B Write the words that tell about more than one thing.

1. life
   _____

2. dish
   _____

3. book
   _____

4. loaf
   _____

5. bench
   _____

6. hiss
   _____

7. knife
   _____

Lesson 53

C Circle the correct meaning of each word.

1. reclaim
   - the opposite of claim
   - claim again

2. disagree
   - the opposite of agree
   - agree again

3. unreal
   - the opposite of real
   - real again

4. untie
   - the opposite of tie
   - tie again

5. rethink
   - the opposite of think
   - think again

6. undress
   - the opposite of dress
   - dress again

7. redo
   - the opposite of do
   - do again

8. disappear
   - the opposite of appear
   - appear again

9. reorder
   - the opposite of order
   - order again

10. disorder
    - the opposite of order
    - order again

END OF LESSON 53

A Use the checks to fix the paragraph.

DID	Emily threw a ball to Robert. Robert jump
CP	up to catch the ball. The ball went over
	Robert's head it rolled down the hill
	toward a skunk. Rover chased the ball.
M	Robert and Emily held their noses.

Check M: Does each sentence tell the main thing?

Check CP: Does each sentence begin with a capital letter and end with a period?

Check DID: Does each sentence tell what somebody or something did?

B Complete each sentence.

> herself   yourself   himself   myself   itself

1. I saw a picture of _____ .

2. Do you feel proud of _____ ?

3. Our cat licked _____ clean.

4. Leo hurt _____ playing ball.

5. Sally thinks she can do the work by _____ .

C Complete the deduction.

Anybody who has squash on their breath ate squash.

The bluebirds have _____

So _____

INDEPENDENT WORK

D **Circle the correct meaning for each word.**

1. disagree
   - the opposite of agree
   - agree again

2. unhappy
   - the opposite of happy
   - happy again

3. remake
   - the opposite of make
   - make again

4. disobey
   - the opposite of obey
   - obey again

5. retake
   - the opposite of take
   - take again

6. unclear
   - the opposite of clear
   - clear again

END OF LESSON 54

55

Name _____

A Complete each sentence.

> myself   yourself   himself
> herself   itself   ourselves   themselves

1. We were sitting by _____ .

2. James was working quietly by _____ .

3. The bird flew by _____ for the first time.

4. The girl locked _____ in the house.

5. Mary and Tia washed _____ in the lake.

6. Tess and I ran by _____ .

7. I read the story aloud to _____ .

8. You can see _____ in the photo.

9. They hurt _____ when they fell.

B Complete the deduction.

- The shoes that fit the footprints made the footprints.

- This shoe _____

So this shoe _____

END OF LESSON 55

A Use the checks to fix the paragraph.

	A little bird fell out of its
DID	nest. James picks up the bird.
M	His sister climbed up the tree. ^
CP	she put the bird back in its nest.

Check M: Does each sentence tell the main thing?

Check CP: Does each sentence begin with a capital letter and end with a period?

Check DID: Does each sentence tell what somebody or something did?

B Complete each sentence.

1. One goose was flying, but all the other _____ were swimming.

   > goose   geese   gooses

2. There were 17 _____ living in the mountains.

   > wolfs   wolf   wolves

3. She filled all the _____ .

   > glasses   glass   glaz

Lesson 56

4. John's brother had two missing _____ .

        (teeth   tooths   tooth)

5. Ann's _____ were very sore.

    (foots   foot   feet)

6. They had only three _____ .

      (match   matchs   matches)

C Complete each sentence.

> myself   yourself   himself
> herself   itself   ourselves   themselves

1. The cat is fighting with _____ in the mirror.

2. The boys were eating by _____ .

3. Can't you figure that out by _____ ?

4. Jessica and I went walking by _____ .

5. Rob hums to _____ as he works.

6. She doesn't like to watch TV by _____ .

7. They told _____ they could do it.

8. Sometimes I talk to _____ .

END OF LESSON 56

57 Name ___

A **Replace the contractions with word pairs.**

The students weren't ready for the test. The teacher hadn't told them that they'd have to answer questions about things they don't like to wear. There wasn't anything that Rodney didn't like to wear. So he couldn't write anything.

B **Write the plural for each word.**

1. woman ___

2. goose ___

3. child ___

4. tooth ___

5. mouse ___

6. man ___

7. foot ___

INDEPENDENT WORK

C **Complete each sentence.**

> myself　　　　yourself　　　　himself
> herself　　　itself　　　　ourselves　　　　themselves

1. Henry went to the store by _____ .

2. I told _____ I could win the race.

3. Rob and Stan sat by _____ .

4. My mom sang to _____ all day long.

5. You can take care of _____ .

D **Write the contraction for each word pair.**

1. you would _____
2. they are _____
3. are not _____
4. what is _____
5. let us _____
6. he is _____
7. she will _____
8. I am _____

END OF LESSON 57

A Circle the correct plural for each word. Then write it.

1. sheep _____
   sheep   sheeps   sheepes

2. loaf _____
   loavs   loafs   loaves

3. mouse _____
   mouse   mice   mouses

4. foot _____
   foot   foots   feet

5. deer _____
   deer   deers   deeres

6. man _____
   men   mans   man

7. class _____
   class   classs   classes

8. child _____
   child   children   childs

9. shelf _____
   shelves   shelfs   shelvs

10. catch _____
    catch   catches   catchs

11. tooth _____
    tooth   tooths   teeth

12. woman _____
    woman   women   womans

B Write the words that tell about each food.

| spicy | cold | hot | sweet | sour |

1. _____ _____

2. _____ _____

3. _____ _____

4. _____ _____

5. _____ _____

C Replace the contractions with word pairs.

The new cars weren't clean, so the leader told us that we'd have to clean them. Some of us couldn't reach the high parts on the car, so we didn't clean those parts. The leader asked, "Where's the long-handled brush?"

I said, "We don't know."

The leader said, "Who's the tallest worker?"

Kelly said, "I'm the tallest."

The leader said, "Then you're the one who's going to wash the roofs."

INDEPENDENT WORK

D **Circle the correct meaning.**

1. resell
   - the opposite of sell
   - sell again

2. dislike
   - the opposite of like
   - like again

3. review
   - the opposite of view
   - view again

4. replay
   - the opposite of play
   - play again

5. uncover
   - the opposite of cover
   - cover again

6. disappear
   - the opposite of appear
   - appear again

END OF LESSON 58

Name _____

59

A Draw a line from each face to the correct word.

1. angry •

2. furious •

3. sad •

4. indifferent •

5. happy •

6. amused •

B **Replace the contractions with word pairs.**

I'm writing this email to complain about the TV we bought from you. It doesn't work. Here's what happened. I plugged it in, but I couldn't turn it on. The on button wouldn't work. It's on now, but it's not working right. It doesn't stay on one channel. It's jumping around from one channel to another. I'm bringing it back to your store tomorrow.

INDEPENDENT WORK

C **Circle the correct plural word. Then write it.**

1. boss _____
   boss   bosss   bosses

2. lash _____
   lash   lashes   lashs

3. deer _____
   deers   deerz   deer

4. dog _____
   dog   dogs   dogges

5. child _____
   children   child   childs

D Complete each sentence.

> myself yourself himself
> herself itself ourselves themselves

1. Bill and I went to the game by _____ .

2. Sue hurt _____ on the stove.

3. We can get _____ up in the morning.

4. I will make _____ some lunch.

5. They cannot teach _____ in the snow.

END OF LESSON 59

60 Name _____

A Use the checks to fix the paragraph.

CP	A truck went over a rock A barrel fell
DID	out of the truck. The barrel rolls down a hill.
EH CP	It crashed into a tree. The boy caught the apple he gave it to a teacher.

Check EH: Tell everything that happened.

Check CP: Begin with a capital letter and end with a period.

Check DID: Tell what somebody or something did.

INDEPENDENT WORK

B Circle the correct plural word. Then write it in the blank.

1. foot _____   foots   foot   feet
2. man _____   mans   men   man
3. sheep _____   sheep   sheeps   sheepes
4. inch _____   inchs   inches   inch
5. book _____   book   bookes   books

END OF LESSON 60

Name _____

61

A **Replace the improper words with proper words.**

give me   police officer   children   surprised   men   dollars

1. A cop was standing on the corner.

2. Five guys helped me clean up the mess.

3. I like those little kids.

4. Who is going to gimme some help with my homework?

5. John needed five bucks more.

6. I was blown away when the coach dunked the ball.

END OF LESSON 61

62

A Use the checks to fix the paragraph.

SP CP	A gorilla escapt from its cage the
	zookeeper made a trail of bananas that led
DID	back to the cage. The gorilla follows the
	zookeeper. The gorilla picked up the bananas
EH	and started to eat them. ∧ The zookeeper
	closed the gate behind the gorilla.

Check EH: Tell everything that happened.

Check SP: Spell words from the word list correctly.

Check CP: Begin with a capital letter and end with a period.

Check DID: Tell what somebody or something did.

B Replace the improper words with proper words.

> bad experience   food   leave   risky   movie

1. We did not like the flick.

2. Her plan is pretty sketchy.

3. Uncle Fred fixed some good grub.

4. We need to cut out of the meeting early.

5. Going to the dentist every week is a bummer.

INDEPENDENT WORK

C Complete each sentence.

> myself   yourself   himself
> herself   itself   ourselves   themselves

1. When can we go by _____ ?

2. I am teaching _____ to play the flute.

3. Bill threw _____ into the pool.

4. Tess and Jill camped by _____ in the park.

5. Molly sang by _____ for the teacher.

END OF LESSON 62

63

A Replace the improper words with proper words.

> disgusting   relax   noise   leave   potatoes

1. Stop making all that racket.

2. Frank looked gross when he spilled paint on his pants.

3. How are you going to cook those taters?

4. It's time to split.

5. My little sister needs to chill out.

B Write the correct plural word in each blank.

1. The _____ were tired.   **wolf**

2. Her _____ were dirty.   **glass**

3. There were lots of _____ at the party.   **child**

4. He forgot to brush his _____ .   **tooth**

5. How many _____ were in line?   **man**

END OF LESSON 63

A Use the checks to fix the paragraph.

SP CP	Alex throow a flying disc to his
	dog the flying disc went over the
	dog's head. A bear cub grabbed the
EH DID	flying disc. ∧ The mother bear heard
	the barking and walks into the field.
CP	Alex picked up his dog and ran away

Check EH: Tell everything that happened.

Check SP: Spell words from the word list correctly.

Check CP: Begin with a capital letter and end with a period.

Check DID: Tell what somebody or something did.

B Replace each contraction. Replace each word that is not proper.

> relax   would   food   noise   dollars
> leave   men   movie   disgusting

We weren't sure where we'd go that day, but we knew we had to get away from the racket on our street. Six guys were fixing some gross holes in the street. It was time for us to split. Vera wanted to see a flick. Burt wanted grub, but I wanted to go someplace and chill out. We had 11 bucks between us, so we couldn't do much. We picked up some cheap grub and went to the park.

C Write the correct plural word in each blank.

1. His _____ were clean.   **shoe**

2. Jon had two new _____.   **watch**

3. The _____ were filled with books.   **shelf**

4. Don't put your _____ on the couch.   **foot**

END OF LESSON 64

Name _____ **65**

A Draw a line from each word to the right picture.

1. run •

2. walk •

3. sprint •

4. creep •

5. jog •

B Write the correct plural word in each blank.

1. The _____ ran across the floor.   **mouse**

2. She liked the teachers in all her _____ .   **class**

3. We caught 11 _____ .   **fish**

4. He made three _____ .   **wish**

END OF LESSON 65

A

1. landing
2. homeland
3. landslide

B Use the checks to fix the paragraph.

DID	The truck driver drived the truck to the
EH	side of the road. She got out of the truck. ^
SP CP	John took the spair tire out of the trunk the
	truck driver jacked up the car. John took
	the flat tire off the car.

Check EH: Tell everything that happened in the middle picture.

Check Sentences: Write all your sentences correctly (**SP, CP, DID**).

C Write the correct plural word in each blank.

1. I don't like to wash _____ . **dish**

2. The room was filled with _____ . **bird**

3. Five _____ walked near our tent. **deer**

4. The _____ were wet. **bench**

INDEPENDENT WORK

D Complete each sentence.

| landing | land | landslide | landlubber | homeland |

1. The heavy rains turned the hillside into a _____ .

2. Jose missed the warmth of his tropical _____ .

3. The airplane made a smooth _____ .

END OF LESSON 66

67 Name _____

A Write the words that tell about each food.

| soft | hard | chewy | crunchy | juicy |

1.
   _____
   _____

2.
   _____
   _____

3.
   _____
   _____

4.
   _____
   _____

5.
   _____
   _____

INDEPENDENT WORK

B Complete each sentence.

| collector | collection | collect | collectible |

1. The beautiful painting was very _____ .

2. The _____ paid a lot of money for the stamp.

3. Mario had a large _____ of seashells.

END OF LESSON 67

A Use the checks to fix the paragraph.

SP	Mr. Wingate swung the net at the
	buttafly. The net missed the butterfly.
EH CP	The mother bear growled. Mr. Wingate ran
	away as fast as he could he ran toward
	a big tree. The mother bear ran after
DID	Mr. Wingate. He is climbing up the tree.

Check EH: Tell everything that happened in the middle picture.

Check Sentences: Write all of your sentences correctly (**SP, CP, DID**).

B HOW THINGS FEEL

1. soft
2. hard
3. crunchy
4. chewy
5. juicy

Lesson 68

C Replace the underlined words with words that are clear.

1.

My brother and my sister had pet pigs. <u>They</u> just loved to roll around in the mud.

2.

We always kept a glass on top of the refrigerator. We kept <u>it</u> full of water.

END OF LESSON 68

Name _____

A Replace the underlined words with words that are clear.

1.

My brother and my sister had pet pigs. <u>They</u> just loved to roll around in the mud.

2.

We always kept a glass on top of the refrigerator. We kept <u>it</u> full of water.

INDEPENDENT WORK

B Complete each sentence.

> activate   actions   act   activity   active

1. My favorite _____ is swimming.

2. Jimmy is very _____ , always doing something.

3. How do you _____ this computer?

4. We did a lot of _____ when playing *Simon Says*.

C Write the word pair for each contraction.

1. haven't

2. you'd

3. they're

4. who's

5. couldn't

6. here's

7. I'm

8. he's

9. we'll

END OF LESSON 69

Name _____ 70

A RELATED WORDS

1. circular
2. circulate
3. circulation

B Use the checks to fix the paragraph.

	Carla rode her bike near the tree. She
EH	got off her bike. The monkey climbed up
	the tree to the tangled string. The monkey
DID	freed the kite. It floats into the air.
CP	Carla wanted to give the monkey a treat
SP	she took some bananas from her baskit.

Check EH: Tell everything that happened in the middle picture.

Check Sentences: Write all of your sentences correctly (**SP, CP, DID**).

Lesson 70

C Change item 1 to tell what Zelda drew. Change item 2 to tell what Mrs. Hudson wanted.

1. Mother held Baby Sarah as she drank from a baby bottle.

2. Mother held Baby Sarah as she drank from a baby bottle.

INDEPENDENT WORK

D Complete each sentence.

> uncomfortable   comforts   comfortable

1. My mom always _____ me when I'm upset.

2. I was _____ under the cozy blanket.

3. The stone in my shoe was very _____ .

END OF LESSON 70

Name _____

A

| 1. hilarious | 2. catastrophic | 3. toxic |

1. He found the story so <u>hilarious</u> that he couldn't stop laughing.

2. We thought the rainstorm would be <u>catastrophic</u>, but it didn't do very much damage.

3. He became very sick from breathing the <u>toxic</u> air in the cave.

INDEPENDENT WORK

B **Complete each sentence.**

| circular | circle | circulates | circulation |

1. The air _____ better when the fan is on.

2. The pan lid was perfectly _____ .

3. We sat in a _____ to hear the story.

4. Molly went to the doctor for her poor _____ .

END OF LESSON 71

72

A Circle the part of each sentence that can be moved.

1. It started to rain at noon.
2. On the way to the game we saw an eagle.
3. For five days he was sick.
4. The water began leaking in the basement.

B Use the checks to fix the paragraph.

	Carlos and Henry decided to go fishing
CP	on Saturday. Their alarm clock rang at 6 in
	the morning the boys sat up. Carlos reached
	to turn off the alarm clock. After a couple
EH	of minutes, the boys got out of bed. They ^
DID	picked up the fishing poles and the net. They
	go outside to wait for their ride. Mr. Lopez
	drove over to the house to pick them up.

Check EH: Tell everything that happened.

Check S: Write all your sentences correctly (**SP, CP, DID**).

END OF LESSON 72

Name _____

A **Circle the part of each sentence that can be moved.**

1. Before the movie we ate dinner.
2. We practiced catching balls in the park.
3. The car almost broke down on the way home.
4. Since he fell he seems unhappy.

B

1. avid   2. fatal   3. optimistic

1. He was such an avid reader that he spent almost all his free time reading.

2. The newspaper called it a fatal accident because three people died.

3. Joe was looking forward to camping this weekend, and he was optimistic that the weather would improve by then.

END OF LESSON 73

A

1. fatal
2. optimistic
3. avid

B Use the checks to fix the paragraph.

CP	Sandra decided to take her dog ice skating at the pond she rode her horse to the pond. Her dog followed the horse.
DID EH	Sandra gets off her horse. She took off her helmet and boots. Then she put
SP	on her skates. Sandra walkd with her dog to the pond.

Check EH: Tell everything that happened.

Check S: Write all your sentences correctly (**SP, CP, DID**).

END OF LESSON 74

Name _____   76

A Circle each picture that shows a group.

1.

2.

3.

4.

5.

6.

Lesson 76   135

B Use the checks to fix the paragraph.

SP	Sally went skating on a frozn pond. She
DID	took her dog Alex with her. Alex falls into
CP	the icy water. he could not climb out of the water. Sally got a board from the barricade.
EH	She held one end of the board. Alex climbed onto the board.

Check EH: Tell everything that happened.

Check S: Write all your sentences correctly (**SP, CP, DID**).

C

1. frantic
2. careful
3. gentle

4. _(handwritten)_
5. day
6. _(handwritten)_
7. _(handwritten)_
8. grow

9. carefully
10. gently
11. frantically

END OF LESSON 76

77

Name _____

A Write the correct name for each group.

> prod   pack   flack   stack
> pick   pride   flock   stick

1. a _____ of lions   2. a _____ of sheep

3. a _____ of dogs   4. a _____ of books

B WORDS THAT TELL WHAT KIND

1. _____ boy   2. _____ dog
3. _____ building   4. _____ story

END OF LESSON 77

Lesson 77

78 Name _____

A Write 7 words in alphabetical order.

1. _____
2. _____
3. _____
4. _____
5. _____
6. _____
7. _____

ball	hot
go	end
dig	ant
fill	ink
candy	

B Use the checks to fix the paragraph.

CP	Fred was painting a chair black he was
	on his back porch. A dog ran onto the
EH	porch to chase the cat. The paint spilled ^
DID	everywhere. It goes on Fred's pants and
CP SP	shoes. fred got a hoze to clean off the dog.

Check EH: Tell everything that happened.

Check S: Write all your sentences correctly (**SP, CP, DID**).

C GROUP NAMES

1. stack   2. flock   3. pride   4. pack

5. swarm   6. team   7. herd   8. crowd   9. forest   10. bunch

D Write the correct name for each group.

1. a large group of people _____

2. a large group of cows _____

3. a group of bananas that grow together _____

4. a large group of flying insects _____

5. a large group of trees _____

6. a group of players _____

E Circle the words that tell what kind.

1. _____ building

   fast   brown   smart   ugly   walking   tall   old   smiling

2. _____ girl

   gold   loud   blue   smiling   pretty   square   plastic   quiet

END OF LESSON 78

Lesson 78

A. Put the words in alphabetical order.

1. _____
2. _____
3. _____
4. _____
5. _____
6. _____
7. _____

> line
> ground
> it
> moon
> help
> kitchen
> jumps

B. Circle the words that tell what kind.

1. _____ story

- sad
- looked
- good
- funny
- green
- me
- new
- head

2. _____ person

- ran
- happy
- looked
- sat
- standing
- lonely
- quickly
- skinny

Lesson 79

C Write the name that tells about each group.

> pride   team   bunch   stack   crowd
> herd   pack   forest   swarm   flock

1. a large group of people _____

2. a large group of trees _____

3. a group of lions _____

4. a pile of coins _____

5. a group of sheep _____

6. a group of players _____

7. a group of cows _____

8. a large group of bees _____

9. a group of flowers that is tied together _____

10. a group of dogs _____

END OF LESSON 79

A Put the words in alphabetical order.

Word box: helpful, jumpy, farmer, inside, knock, gate, landed

1. _____
2. _____
3. _____
4. _____
5. _____
6. _____
7. _____

B NAMES OF GROUPS

1. herd
2. bunch
3. pride
4. forest
5. flock
6. team
7. crowd
8. swarm

- school
- army
- fleet

C Write the correct name for each item.

> pack　　fleet　　team　　flock　　school
> forest　　swarm　　crowd　　stack　　army

1. a group of players _____

2. a group of birds _____

3. a large group of wasps _____

4. a group of soldiers _____

5. a group of wolves _____

6. a large group of people _____

7. a group of ships _____

8. a pile of books _____

9. a group of fish _____

10. a large group of trees _____

INDEPENDENT WORK

D Write the words that tell what kind of book.

> good   walking   talked   old
> slowly   red   smiles   new

• _____ book   • _____ book

• _____ book   • _____ book

E Circle the correct plural word. Then write it in the blank.

1. dish _____   dishs   dishes   dish
2. man _____   men   mans   mens
3. foot _____   foots   feet   feets
4. shelf _____   shelvs   shelfs   shelves
5. path _____   paths   pathes   pathz
6. fox _____   foxs   foxez   foxes

END OF LESSON 80

Name _____

A Put the words in alphabetical order.

a b c d e f g h i j k l m n o p q r s t u v w x y z

1. _____
2. _____
3. _____
4. _____
5. _____
6. _____
7. _____

- jaws
- lake
- nothing
- ice
- oldest
- kitten
- meaning

B Circle words that tell <u>when</u> or <u>how</u>.

1. **ran**

   quickly
   old
   pillow
   often
   yesterday
   pretty

2. **talked**

   fast
   phone
   lonely
   table
   quietly
   white
   slowly

Lesson 81   145

C Write the correct name for each picture: Zelda or Henry.

1. Three little boys picked strawberries. They were as big as apples.

_____ _____

2. Before the children pulled up the tulips, my sister watered them with the hose.

_____ _____

END OF LESSON 81

Name _____

A Put the words in alphabetical order.

a b c d e f g h i j k l m n o p q r s t u v w x y z

1. _____
2. _____
3. _____
4. _____
5. _____
6. _____
7. _____

restful
pound
older
something
question
until
thing

B Circle the correct word for each sentence.

1. The group of people was / were shouting.

2. The army of ants moves / move fast.

3. The pride of lions are / is resting.

4. The forest of trees gives / give shade.

5. The fleet of ships look / looks good.

END OF LESSON 82

Lesson 82 147

A Write the correct word in each blank.

house   young   fence   quickly   green

1. The _____ boy ran _____ .

any   look   small   under   fast   swinging

2. Those _____ ducks like to swim _____ .

tall   under   large   paper   well   never   life

3. He sang _____ in front of a _____ crowd.

B Put the words in alphabetical order.

a b c d e f g h i j k l m n o p q r s t u v w x y z

1. _____
2. _____
3. _____
4. _____
5. _____
6. _____
7. _____

wishful
time
zoo
yawning
ugly
x-ray
van

C Complete each sentence.

1. The crowd of fans   was / were   cheering.

2. Her stack of coins   grow / grows   every day.

3. That flock of geese   flies / fly   north every spring.

4. The forest of pine trees   are / is   pretty.

INDEPENDENT WORK

D Put these words in alphabetical order. Word 1 is muffin.

1. _____
2. _____
3. _____
4. _____
5. _____
6. _____
7. _____
8. _____

- offices
- muffin
- rest
- toolbox
- name
- quiz
- soap
- prize

END OF LESSON 83

84

Name _____

A Complete the letter.

| zoo | friends | class | family |

Dear _____ ,

    Yesterday, I went to the _____ with my _____ . We saw _____ , _____ , and _____ . My favorite animals were the _____ . I hope that I can go back to the _____ soon.

    From,

_____

B Write the correct word in each blank.

| house   slowly   talking   always   old   large |

1. A _____ dog walked _____ to the fence.

| cat   alone   running   quickly   happy   tall   book |

2. A _____ tree stood _____ in the field.

| fed   all   quickly   ate   burning   told   happy |

3. The people ran _____ from the _____ building.

C Circle the correct word for each sentence.

1. The army of ants moves / move very fast.

2. The stack of books get / gets taller every day.

3. That pile of sticks look / looks smaller than it had been.

4. The herd of cows is / are walking back to the farm.

Lesson 84   151

INDEPENDENT WORK

D Put these words in alphabetical order. Word 1 is <u>enjoy</u>.

1. _____
2. _____
3. _____
4. _____
5. _____
6. _____
7. _____
8. _____

key
itch
enjoy
gets
felt
limp
half
jeans

E Capitalize each sentence.

1. the woodburn zoo is closed on new year's day.

2. my sister tess has a birthday next monday.

3. the hottest month in newton is july.

4. what day comes after friday and before sunday?

END OF LESSON 84

Name _____

A   Complete the letter.

birthday   paint set   football   kite   book

play games

eat cake

go swimming

Dear _____ ,

　　Next week, I will be _____ years old. I am going to have a _____ party. My friends and I will _____ and _____ . The birthday present I want most is a _____ . I hope I get it.

　　From,

　　_____

B Circle the words that tell what happened. Then complete each item.

What Kind
green helpful
furry hot

How
loudly safely
slowly

1. _____ teacher _____
2. _____ yelled _____
3. _____ walked _____
4. _____ cat _____
5. _____ drove _____
6. _____ flame _____
7. _____ book _____

INDEPENDENT WORK

C Circle the correct word for each sentence.

1. Our football team plays / play every week.

2. The crowd of fans are / is yelling for their team.

3. This bunch of grapes taste / tastes good.

4. The flock of birds was / were flying north.

END OF LESSON 85

154 Lesson 85

Name _____

86

A Complete the letter.

school   go for walks   grandma's   the park

dog

cat

 fish  parrot

 bunny

turtle

hamster

snake

Dear _____ ,

    The pet that I would like the most is a _____ . I would name my pet _____ , and I would take care of my _____ . We would have a lot of fun together.

    I would take my pet to _____ and _____ . I would love my _____ and my _____ would love me.

From,

_____

Lesson 86   155

B Choose a good word for each item.

What Kind	How
weak tasty	sadly slowly
gold new	easily

1. _____ opens _____

2. _____ wins _____

3. _____ horse _____

4. _____ talks _____

5. _____ food _____

6. _____ coin _____

INDEPENDENT WORK

C Write the correct name for each group.

pride	stack	herd	flock
crowd	swarm	forest	school

1. a _____ of sheep

2. a _____ of lions

3. a _____ of people

4. a _____ of bees

END OF LESSON 86

Name _____

A Complete the letter.

Dear _____ ,
    Here are a few of my favorite things. My favorite things to eat are _____ and _____ . My favorite things to do are _____ and _____ . My favorite people are _____ and _____ .
    From,
_____

Lesson 87

B Use the checks to fix the paragraph.

CP	Mrs. Hart was walking down a hill with
	her dog her dog was walking right behind her.
DID	Suddenly Mrs. Hart was tripping over a rock.
	Her dog stopped and watched her. Mrs. Hart
DID	rolled down the hill toward a cliff. The dog
SP	will run after her. Mrs. Hart rolled to the edje
	of the cliff. Then her dog grabbed Mrs. Hart's
	coat and held onto her.

Check WAS: Does the first part of your story tell what Mrs. Hart **was doing** and what her dog **was doing?**

Check DID: Do the rest of your sentences tell what Mrs. Hart **did** and what her dog **did?**

C

1. Then   2. Suddenly

D Write the correct word for each item.

Then   Suddenly

1. The clock was working well.

   It stopped all at once.

   _____ it stopped.

2. Robert finished his schoolwork.

   He played catch with his sister next.

   _____ he played catch with his sister.

3. Jane was sitting on a rock.

   She fell off the rock all at once.

   _____ she fell off the rock.

4. Our dog was sleeping.

   He woke up all at once.

   _____ he woke up.

5. The sky was cloudy.

   The clouds began to move away next.

   _____ the clouds began to move away.

INDEPENDENT WORK

E Put these words in alphabetical order. Word 1 is join.

1. _____
2. _____
3. _____
4. _____
5. _____
6. _____
7. _____

- long
- noise
- kite
- mouse
- orange
- join
- poke

F Complete each sentence.

1. The pride of lions   were / was   out hunting.

2. My stack of books   fill / fills   the shelf.

3. A swarm of bees   has / have   its hive close by.

4. The forest of trees   is / are   very large.

160   Lesson 87

G Write the correct word in each blank.

| soon | old | ate | quietly | yours |

1. My _____ dog sat _____ all day long.

| empty | wildly | sunshine | such | loudly | curly |

2. Ruth's _____ hair blew _____ in the wind.

| fast | paper | bad | loudly | ready |

3. Ben cried _____ when he heard the _____ news.

| empty | great | sweetly | purple | sick | madly |

4. She sang _____ to the _____ boy.

END OF LESSON 87

88 Name _____

A Complete the letter.

- a vacation
- a castle
- a skateboard
- a friend
- a horse
- a magic wand
- money

three wishes

Dear _____ ,
   This is what I would wish for if I had _____
_____ . First I would wish for
_____ . Next I would wish
for _____ . Last I would
wish for _____ .
   From,
   _____

B Circle all the words that belong on this page.

shirt	s t u v	velvet
shirt		soil
sop		yesterday
prank		umbrella
rent		velvet
vase		

C Write the correct word for each sentence.

> Then   Suddenly

1. The bus was going 30 miles per hour. The bus stopped all at once.

   _____ the bus stopped.

2. We were watching TV. The lights went out all at once.

   _____ the lights went out.

3. The pie cooled for half an hour. We ate it next.

   _____ we ate it.

4. We walked to the corner.
   Next we waited over ten minutes for the bus.

   _____ we waited over ten minutes for the bus.

5. Mr. Anderson walked up his front steps.
   He slipped all at once and almost fell.

   _____ he slipped and almost fell.

END OF LESSON 88

Lesson 88   163

A Circle all the words that belong on this page.

halt   h i j k l m   mustard

- halt
- longer
- keel
- faith
- insect
- lovely

- hope
- mule
- cat
- kitten
- pun
- mustard

B Punctuate the letter.

May 6 2015

Dear Fran

    we lost our dog at the beach we searched and searched but couldn't find her we finally went back to our car there she was, sitting next to the car

    Your pal

    Jenny

C **Write the correct word for each sentence.**

> Finally   Then   Suddenly

1. The goat was stuck in the mud. He tried and tried to get out.

   After a long time he got out of the mud.

   _____ he got out of the mud.

2. Four monkeys and a cat were sitting on a branch.

   All at once the branch broke.

   _____ the branch broke.

3. A red truck stopped at the corner.

   A green truck stopped at the corner next.

   _____ a green truck stopped at the corner.

4. We stood by the stove for more than ten minutes.

   At last mom opened the oven and took out the pie.

   _____ mom opened the oven and took out the pie.

5. First she took the clothes out of the washing machine.

   She dried the clothes next.

   _____ she dried the clothes.

END OF LESSON 89

90 Name _____

A Add commas where they belong.

March 11 2018

Dear Ben

_____

_____

_____

Your friend

Marco

B Write the correct word in each sentence.

| Finally | Then | Suddenly |

1. Ann was walking next to her house.

   _____ her brother jumped out and scared her.

2. Dan lost two teeth last month.

   _____ he lost another tooth this month.

3. Linda waited three hours at the airport.

   _____ her mother's plane arrived.

4. The balloon floated over to the fence.

   _____ it popped!

INDEPENDENT WORK

C Write the correct word in each blank.

| water | sailor | large | wavy | quickly | tomorrow |

1. The _____ ship sailed _____ out to sea.

| old | green | lively | loudly | girl | yes |

2. I talked _____ so the _____ man could hear me.

| song | slowly | together | many | tricky | usual |

3. Mike played _____ because it was a _____ tune.

| two | safely | my | best | music | widely |

4. Her _____ friend drives _____ .

D Choose the correct name for each group.

1. the _____ of birds
2. a _____ of trees
3. that _____ of cows
4. this _____ of ants

forest	army
crowd	school
herd	flock
pride	team

END OF LESSON 90

A Write the date, the greeting, and the closing for the letter that Bonnie wrote.

_____

_____

_____

_____

B Write the correct word for each sentence.

| Finally | Then | Suddenly |

1. The children stayed up very late watching TV.

   _____ they went to bed.

2. The rabbit didn't move as we walked toward it.

   _____ it jumped up and ran out of the barn.

3. Martha read the book for more than five months.

   _____ she finished it.

4. Jim walked into the room and picked up a paper.

   _____ he sat on the couch.

END OF LESSON 91

Name _____

92

A Fix up the report so it names the right people and things.

Molly Henderson

Angelo / accordion

It Folds Up

It was regular-sized with two full-sized wheels. Then it folded up to the size of a book. She said, "I got the idea when I talked to him. It became bigger and smaller when he played it."

B Write the date, the greeting, and the closing for the letter that Pedro wrote.

_____

_____

_____

_____

INDEPENDENT WORK

C Write the correct name for each group.

| pride | school | army | bunch |
| herd | team | pack | flock |

1. a _____ of players

2. a _____ of bananas

3. a _____ of dogs

4. a _____ of fish

END OF LESSON 92

Name _____

A Replace the unclear words.

	Linda Jackson was at it. She was digging in it.
	She found them. She sold them.

INDEPENDENT WORK

B Circle the correct word.

1. My bunch of bananas look / looks ripe.

2. The crowd of people is / are coming closer.

3. The school of fish swims / swim together.

4. The army of ants eat / eats all the crops.

5. Your stack of coins was / were bigger than mine.

END OF LESSON 95

Lesson 95 171

Name _____

A **Find the meaning of the underlined words in your glossary.**

1. The ship carried a <u>crate</u> of coconuts.

2. The queen's behavior gave the prince the wrong <u>impression</u>.

3. The Rangers won the football game with a <u>field goal</u>.

INDEPENDENT WORK

B **Write the correct name for each group.**

> school   flock   bunch   army   forest   team
> crowd   pride   swarm   pack   stack

1. a _____ of people

2. the _____ of flowers

3. the _____ of trees

4. that _____ of bees

5. the _____ of ants

6. his _____ of sheep

7. a _____ of players

END OF LESSON 99

Name _____

A Find the meaning of the underlined words in your glossary.

1. She didn't want to let her friends down.

2. The palace was on top of a beautiful hill.

3. His watch was very valuable.

B

END OF LESSON 100

101

A Put 8 in the box for Rolla. Then number all the other horses.

END OF LESSON 101

Name _____

102

A 1 is in the box for Rolla. Number all the other horses.

END OF LESSON 102

Lesson 102 **175**

103   Name _____

A Put the words in alphabetical order.

a b c d e f g h i j k l m n o p q r s t u v w x y z

1. _____
2. _____
3. _____
4. _____
5. _____
6. _____

- should
- length
- yellow
- older
- umbrella
- jail

INDEPENDENT WORK

B Circle the correct word for each sentence.

1. The bunch of grapes   taste / tastes   good.

2. The school of fish   moves / move   quickly.

3. A crowd of workers   are / is   eating lunch.

4. The pack of wolves   were / was   tired.

END OF LESSON 103

Name _____

104

A Put the words in alphabetical order.

a b c d e f g h i j k l m n o p q r s t u v w x y z

1. _____
2. _____
3. _____
4. _____
5. _____
6. _____

monkey
don't
ink
only
answer
happen

INDEPENDENT WORK

B Write the correct name for each group.

stack   team   bunch   pride
   crowd   herd   forest   pack

1. a _____ of flowers

2. a _____ of pine trees

3. a _____ of lions

4. a _____ of people

5. a _____ of coins

6. a _____ of basketball players

END OF LESSON 104

Lesson 104   177

105   Name _____

A   Put the words in alphabetical order.

a b c d e f g h i j k l m n o p q r s t u v w x y z

1. _____
2. _____
3. _____
4. _____
5. _____

coat

climb

canned

curly

crazy

B   Put the words in alphabetical order.

a b c d e f g h i j k l m n o p q r s t u v w x y z

1. _____
2. _____
3. _____
4. _____
5. _____

mirror

myna

metal

money

machine

END OF LESSON 105

Name _____

106

A Put the words in alphabetical order.

a b c d e f g h i j k l m n o p q r s t u v w x y z

1. _____
2. _____
3. _____
4. _____
5. _____

officer
outfit
oven
ocean
once

B Circle the correct word for each sentence.

1. A group of ducks   were / was   swimming near the shore.

2. A swarm of bees   is / are   flying above the house.

3. A fleet of big ships   moves / move   slowly.

4. The pack of wolves   are / is   going quietly up the hill.

END OF LESSON 106

Lesson 106   179

107 Name _____

A Put the words in alphabetical order.

a b c d e f g h i j k l m n o p q r s t u v w x y z

1. _____
2. _____
3. _____
4. _____
5. _____
6. _____

squirrel
scale
solid
steady
smelly
shelves

B Circle the correct word for each sentence.

1. A pride of lions were / was resting in the shade.

2. The army of soldiers marches / march together.

3. Our team of players is / are winning the game.

4. The flock of sheep make / makes a lot of noise.

END OF LESSON 107

Name _____

A Put the words in alphabetical order.

a b c d e f g h i j k l m n o p q r s t u v w x y z

1. _____
2. _____
3. _____
4. _____
5. _____
6. _____
7. _____
8. _____

- edge
- enormous
- easy
- evening
- escape
- eggs
- eyes
- eraser

B Spell each word correctly.

1. buket _____
2. trubel _____
3. scool _____

END OF LESSON 109

Lesson 109 **181**

A Draw a line from each picture to the right number.

Life Cycle of a Frog

1. •   •

2. •   •

3. •   •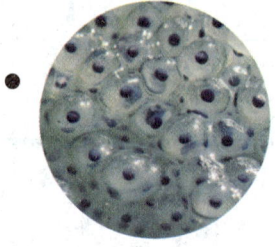

4. •   •

5. •   •

B Circle the correct meaning.

1. macaw

   They saw a <u>macaw</u> in the jungle.
   - large tree
   - colorful bird
   - kind of pond

2. receptacle

   There were lots of <u>receptacles</u> on the table.
   - leftovers
   - papers
   - containers

3. raiment

   Their <u>raiment</u> was stolen.
   - luggage
   - clothing
   - pet

C Spell each word correctly.

1. aksident _____
2. qwiet _____
3. jentel _____
4. payper _____

INDEPENDENT WORK

D Circle the correct word for each sentence.

1. A swarm of bees are / is in the tree.

2. A herd of cows stands / stand in the field.

3. The stack of bricks were / was falling over.

4. A forest of oak trees are / is chopped down every day.

END OF LESSON 110

Lesson 110 183

111 Name _____

A Circle the correct meaning.

1. sanction

   The mayor **sanctioned** our plan.
   - approved
   - fought
   - ignored

2. velocity

   The plane had a lot of **velocity**.
   - fuel
   - passengers
   - speed

3. diminutive

   His daughter was quite **diminutive**.
   - pretty
   - small
   - quiet

B Spell each word correctly.

1. botel _____
2. Munday _____
3. acshin _____

INDEPENDENT WORK

C Write the letters that words on each page could begin with.

1. home .... look _____

2. people .... stay _____

END OF LESSON 111

184 Lesson 111

A **Circle the correct meaning.**

1. Her grandfather had a large <u>residence</u>.
   - television
   - house
   - automobile

2. Sara bought a <u>bassoon</u>.
   - fish
   - musical instrument
   - expensive stone

3. Jinny was never <u>punctual</u>.
   - on time
   - happy
   - lazy

B **Write a report on lined paper.**

Koala Bears

Koala bears ▓▓▓▓▓▓▓▓▓. Koalas ▓▓▓▓▓▓▓▓▓.

▓▓▓▓▓▓▓▓▓▓▓▓▓▓▓▓▓▓▓▓▓▓▓▓▓.

▓▓▓▓▓▓▓▓▓▓▓▓▓▓▓▓▓▓. The thing we found most interesting is ▓▓▓▓▓▓▓.

C **Find the meaning of the underlined words in an online dictionary.**

1. The accident will <u>hold up</u> the traffic for at least an hour.

2. Ted is so tired that he's going to <u>conk out</u> when he gets home.

END OF LESSON 113

115 Name _____

A Circle the correct meaning.

1. We had <u>mullet</u> for dinner.
   - a vegetable   • a fish   • a fruit

2. His mother is an <u>aviator</u>.
   - pilot   • doctor   • nurse

B IMPORTANT WORDS

1. female
2. Australia
3. hatch
4. male
5. dinosaur
6. crocodile
7. pointed
8. Africa
9. dangerous
10. saltwater

INDEPENDENT WORK

C Write the correct name for each group.

1. a _____ of birds
2. the _____ of dogs
3. that _____ of fish
4. the _____ of people
5. a _____ of bees

> crowd
> swarm
> bunch
> pack
> stack
> flock
> school

END OF LESSON 115

Name _____

116

A **Circle the correct meaning.**

1. We could see fish in the <u>shoal</u>.

   • shallow water   • dirty water   • deep water

2. My dad planted a <u>poplar</u> in our yard.

   • flower   • shrub   • tree

B **Say a long sentence for each item.**

END OF LESSON 116

117 Name _____

A Circle the correct meaning.

1. The group walked toward the portal of the zoo.
   • exit   • center   • entrance

2. I intend to go to the movie tonight.
   • hope   • plan   • saved

B Find the meaning of the red words.

1. You take after your mother. She's a good cook.

2. We didn't eat much all day, so we planned to pig out at dinner.

END OF LESSON 117

Name _____ 121

A Write the letter of the picture that shows the correct meaning.

1. The <u>bark</u> was so loud it scared Irma. ___
2. The <u>bark</u> of the birch tree is very smooth. ___
3. The <u>fly</u> landed on Ted's nose. ___
4. She is learning to <u>fly</u> a plane. ___

A.   B.   C.   D.

B Put the words in order from the driest to the wettest.

1. _____
2. _____
3. _____
4. _____

saturated
wet
damp
soaked

END OF LESSON 121

122 Name _____

A Put the words in order from the driest to the wettest.

1. _____
2. _____
3. _____
4. _____

- soaked
- wet
- saturated
- damp

B Complete each item.

| wet | damp | saturated | soaked |

1. He wiped the table with a _____ washcloth.

2. By late evening her towel was not completely dry. It was still _____ .

3. The sponge was in the water overnight so it was completely _____ .

4. When they came home from a walk in the heavy rain, their hair was _____ .

END OF LESSON 122

Name _____

TEST 1

1 **For each sentence circle <u>reports</u> or <u>does not report</u>.**

1. Gary's table had four legs. — reports   does not report

2. Carl poured soup into a pot. — reports   does not report

3. Ramon cooked food over the fire. — reports   does not report

4. The cowboys were very hungry. — reports   does not report

5. Gary used a knife to cut the potato. — reports   does not report

6. The horses belonged to Gary. — reports   does not report

7. The soup smelled good. — reports   does not report

8. Ramon and Carl wore hats. — reports   does not report

TEST 1

2 Next to each word, write the word that tells what people did.

1. tell _____   5. run _____
2. have _____   6. go _____
3. wear _____   7. sit _____
4. see _____

3 Circle the part of each sentence that names. Underline the part that tells more.

1. My brother and my sister were at school.
2. A glass fell off the table.
3. He liked to look at horses.
4. A girl and a boy fixed the fence.
5. They painted the room.

Mastery Test 1

4 Copy each sentence the way it is written.

1. The workers worked for 12 days.

2. Who is ready to run a race?

3. How long will this trip take?

5 Complete the second sentence and the conclusion.

1. All trees have leaves.

2. A _____ is a tree.

   So a _____

   | pine | maple | fir | birch | spruce |

END OF TEST 1

Name _____

TEST **2**

1 Write the words that tell what people did.

1. fly _____
2. give _____
3. stand _____
4. have _____
5. run _____

6. dig _____
7. go _____
8. find _____
9. wear _____
10. tell _____

2 Fix the wrong word in each sentence.

1. The kids standed in line for lunch.

2. The big eagle flied from tree to tree.

3. The dog dugged a hole in the yard.

4. My mom goed to the bank to get some cash.

5. The teacher gaved us a pizza party.

6. How many kids weared gloves?

TEST 2

3. Fix up four sentences in the paragraph.

My friends are going to the park. They are having a good time. Two girls played on the swings. A boy chased a butterfly. A boy and a girl are running in the grass. Everybody is staying in the park until the sun went down.

Check DID: Does each sentence tell what people did?

4. Fill in the blanks with He, She, or It.

1. His shirt was red and blue. _____ had stripes.

2. My mother helped me do my homework. _____ is very good at math.

3. His brother is one year old. _____ can almost walk.

4. My sister went to school. _____ was the first person in the classroom.

5. Circle the subject of each sentence.

Alex taught his pet monkey to do many tricks. The monkey even learned how to ride a bicycle. Alex dressed his monkey in a costume one day. Alex and his monkey went to the circus. They showed a clown their tricks. The clown gave the monkey a job in the circus.

Mastery Test 2

6 Write the letter of each picture that shows what the sentence says.

A.

B.

C.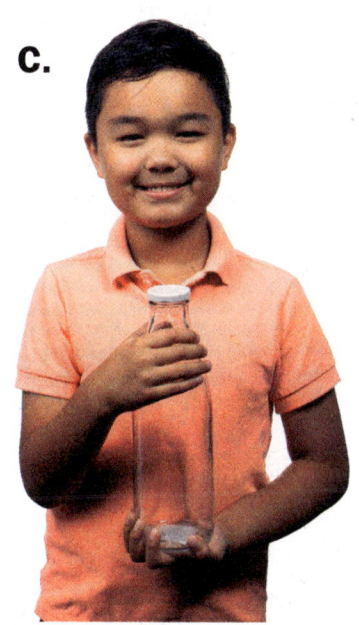

D.

1. He held a bottle. _____

2. A person held a container. _____

3. She held a container. _____

4. He held a container. _____

END OF TEST 2

Name _____

TEST 3

1 Circle the sentence that tells the main thing the group did.

One child could not go fast.

Two children were having fun.

The children rode their bikes.

One bike was new.

2 Write the compound word for each picture.

| fish | basket | dog | arm |
| house | chair | bowl | ball |

1.

   _____

2.

   _____

3.

   _____

4.

   _____

Mastery Test 3 T-9

TEST 3

3 For each item, write **day**, **month**, or **name**.

1. Wednesday _____   5. Monday _____
2. July _____   6. September _____
3. Mr. Jones _____   7. Bonnie Smith _____
4. March _____

4 Fix up any sentences in the paragraph that should name **He**, **She**, or **It**.

Bill went to the bank. Bill needed some cash. The bank was closed. The bank would open the next day. Bill decided to get money the next day. So that's what he did. Mandy was the bank teller at the bank. Mandy gave Bill $200 in cash.

5 Copy the paragraph. Then check your work.

Fran found a shoe. Then she found a sock. Then she found a hat. What did she find next?

Check CP: Does each sentence begin with a capital letter and end with a period?

Check SP: Did you spell each word correctly?

Mastery Test 3

TEST 3

6 Write a sentence that reports on the main thing each animal did. Then check your work.

1.

2.

swam   chewed   ran   climbed   meal

1. _____

2. _____

Check CP: Does each sentence begin with a capital letter and end with a period?

Check M: Does each sentence tell the main thing the animal did?

Check SP: Did you spell the words from the word list correctly?

END OF TEST 3

TEST 4

1 **Fix up each person's name so all parts of the name begin with a capital letter.**

1. jane cristion
2. her uncle
3. mr. holland
4. that tall woman
5. his brother
6. hellen troy
7. mrs. holmes
8. a small boy
9. two sisters

2 **Put in the missing capital letters.**

1. I gave my friend milton chocolates for valentine's day.
2. sue and jane play softball on fridays.
3. when jude eats fizzballs, his lips turn green.
4. In july, we buy glowshow fireworks for independence day.

Mastery Test 4

TEST 4

3. Rewrite each underlined part so it has a word with an apostrophe.

1. The car that belongs to Tom is new.

   _____ is new.

2. Water dripped onto the table that belongs to Ray.

   Water dripped onto _____ .

3. A boy sat on the knee that belongs to his mom.

   A boy sat on _____ .

4. Put apostrophes in the words that need them.

1. her mothers shoes
2. those puppies near the barn
3. my dads new hats
4. I saw Mr. Johnsons living room.
5. We took the boats on the lake.
6. Anns four books
7. lots of plants
8. the bags handle

5 **Fill in the blanks with He, She, It, or They.**

1. Two girls ate lunch. _____ ate lunch.

2. A cow and a horse slept in the barn. _____ slept in the barn.

3. His sister went home. _____ went home.

4. The blue pen fell off the desk. _____ fell off the desk.

5. James is sick today. _____ is sick today.

6. My friends went to a party. _____ went to a party.

6 **Put in the missing capital letters and periods.**

They didn't know what was in the box Fran picked up the box she said it was very light Robert opened it and looked inside he found out it was empty.

END OF TEST 4

Mastery Test 4

Name _____

TEST 5

1 Write the contraction below each word pair.

1. there is _____
2. would not _____
3. you would _____
4. let us _____
5. I am _____
6. can not _____

2 Fix up the run-on sentences.

1. The snow started coming down on Wednesday and it kept snowing through the night and then it snowed more on the next day. (3)

2. We started to get worried by Friday and then it kept snowing and now the snow was over three feet deep. (3)

3 Put in the missing capital letters and periods.

The first thing we did on sunday was walk along the beach my sister and tom wanted to keep walking terry wanted to climb the big hill. on monday my mom wanted to go shopping in the city of portland.

Mastery Test 5

TEST 5

4 Rewrite the paragraph so the underlined parts give a clear picture.

woman
cactus
motorcycle
young
desert
wheel
mountain lion

She was riding a vehicle. She was in the middle of it. An animal jumped in front of it. She turned sharply. The vehicle ran into a plant. The plant damaged it.

_____ was riding a _____ .

She was in the middle of _____ .

_____ jumped in front of _____ .

She turned sharply. _____ ran into a

_____ . _____ damaged

_____ .

END OF TEST 5

T-18   Mastery Test 5

Name _____

TEST 6

1 Circle the correct meaning of each word.

1. unlock
   - the opposite of lock
   - lock again

2. redo
   - the opposite of do
   - do again

3. untie
   - the opposite of tie
   - tie again

4. rewrite
   - the opposite of write
   - write again

5. refill
   - the opposite of fill
   - fill again

6. disobey
   - the opposite of obey
   - obey again

2 Circle each correct plural word. Then write it in the blank.

1. knife _____ knifes   knives   knivs
2. wish _____   wishs   wishes   wish
3. class _____ classes   classz   class
4. lamp _____   lampes   lamp   lamps
5. child _____ childs   childrens children
6. tooth _____ teeth   tooths   toothes

Mastery Test 6   T-19

3 **Complete each sentence.**

> myself   yourself   himself
> herself   itself   ourselves   themselves

1. Richard turned _____ around.

2. My baby sister walked by _____ today.

3. Tod and Tina checked _____ in the mirror.

4. You could do it _____ .

5. The cub sat by _____ in the snow.

6. We finished the job by _____ .

END OF TEST 6

Name _____

TEST 7

1 Write the words that tell about each food.

| soft | hard | chewy | juicy | crunchy |

1.

_____

_____

2.

_____

_____

3.

_____

_____

4.

_____

_____

5.

_____

_____

Mastery Test 7 T-21

TEST 7

2. Draw a line from each word to the right picture.

1. creep •

2. walk •

3. sprint •

4. jog •

3. Underline the root part of each word.

1. circle
   circulate
   circular
   circulation

2. collection
   collector
   collectible

3. action
   activity
   activate

4. comfort
   comfortable
   uncomfortable

T-22 Mastery Test 7

4 Replace each contraction. Then replace each word that is not proper.

| dollars | disgusting | relaxed | police | food |
| noise | leave | men | movie | officers |

We were in school when we heard this terrible racket. We looked out the windows. It was like something you'd see in an action flick. There were cop cars all over and a lot of guys yelling. Two guys were trying to split. They're part of a gang that tried to take 500 bucks and some chow from the bakery, but the cops stopped them before they reached the street. The owner of the bakery gave the chow to the officers. He's glad they were close by.

TEST 7

5 Write a good paragraph that tells everything that happened.

| flying disc | threw | field | Alex | bushes |
| bear | cub | mother | appeared | grabbed |

END OF TEST 7

T-24 Mastery Test 7

Name _____ TEST 8

1 Use the check letters to fix the paragraph.

| accident | through | police officer | happened | driving |

CP	Mrs. Kelly was driving too fast she
CP	did not see the red light. she drove
EH	right past it. The other driver was
DID	mad. A police officer comes by to see
SP	what happend.

TEST 8

2 **Circle the part of each sentence that can move. Then rewrite each sentence.**

1. After dinner we did our homework.
   _____

2. We saw a raccoon in the basement.
   _____

3. We waited until the rain stopped.
   _____

4. In the distance we saw the car coming.
   _____

3 **Circle the words that could tell what kind of day.**

▬▬▬▬▬▬ day

sunny

ran

fun

easily

him

frosty

sister

busy

4. Write the correct name for each group.

> pack   fleet   team   flock
> school   forest   swarm   stack

1. a _____ of insects

2. a _____ of fish

3. a _____ of dogs

4. a _____ of geese

5. a _____ of ships

6. a _____ of books

END OF TEST 8

Name _____   **TEST 9**

1 Circle the correct word for each sentence.

1. The group of children was / were happy.

2. A school of yellow fish stay / stays in shallow water.

3. A flock of sheep is / are eating.

4. That crowd of people look / looks very large.

2 Put these words in alphabetical order.

a b c d e f g h i j k l m n o p q r s t u v w x y z

- joint
- igloo
- leans
- hips
- mud
- kitchen

1. _____
2. _____
3. _____
4. _____
5. _____
6. _____

Mastery Test 9   T-29

3 | **Complete each sentence with the best word.**

| Then | Finally | Suddenly |

1. The bear was very quiet. _____ it roared.

2. The bear slowly opened its eyes. _____ it slowly turned its head.

3. We stood in line for nearly an hour. _____ the line began to move.

4. We were driving at night. _____ a deer jumped in front of our car.

4 | **Write the correct word in each blank.**

| man   quickly   green   tree   brown   tomorrow |

1. A _____ horse jumped _____ over the fence.

| brick   away   happy   loudly   street   over |

2. Those _____ girls could not stop laughing _____ .

| rainbow   ran   wet   slowly   shoes   see |

3. They walked home _____ on a _____ sidewalk.

END OF TEST 9

Name _____

TEST 10

1 Write the date, the greeting, and the closing for your letter to Molly.

> Your friend   April 12   2010

_____

_____

_____

_____

2 Write all the letters that words on each page can begin with.

1. boast   fix   _____

2. pipe   shadow _____

3. heave   lost   _____

4. toast   vest   _____

Mastery Test 10   T-31

TEST 10

3 Write the meaning of each underlined word. Use the glossary at the back of your textbook.

1. We hope the snow will <u>thaw</u> tomorrow.
   _____

2. The story was so <u>dull</u> I could hardly listen to it.
   _____

3. They did not follow the <u>rule</u> about walking quietly.
   _____

4. The ship lost its way in <u>foul</u> weather.
   _____

END OF TEST 10

Name _____

TEST 11

1 **Write your opinion about a good job.**

A Job I Would Like to Have

- **Tell about the job you would like.**
- **Give two reasons why you would like that job.**

I hope ▬▬▬▬▬▬▬▬▬▬▬▬▬▬▬ .

Mastery Test 11   **T-33**

TEST 11

2 **Put these words in alphabetical order.**

a b c d e f g h i j k l m n o p q r s t u v w x y z

1. _____
2. _____
3. _____
4. _____
5. _____
6. _____

jump
radio
egg
music
paper
band

3 **Put these words in alphabetical order. Use the second letter of each word.**

a b c d e f g h i j k l m n o p q r s t u v w x y z

1. _____
2. _____
3. _____
4. _____
5. _____
6. _____

potato
party
person
play
pull
pint

Mastery Test 11

4 Use an online dictionary. Circle the correct meaning of each underlined word.

1. The room was dingy.

    • dark and dirty   • a small boat   • shaped like a bell

2. She saw a large ibex on the hill.

    • a wild flower   • a wild goat   • a rock

3. The sticks would not ignite.

    • catch fire   • break   • float

5 Use an online spell checker. Write the correct spelling for each word.

1. bayker   _____

2. lafter   _____

3. muther   _____

4. stayshun _____

END OF TEST 11

Name _____

TEST 12

1 **Look up the meaning of each underlined word. Then circle the correct meaning.**

1. Do not <u>slumber</u> when the teacher is talking.

    • eat   • sleep   • argue

2. They could not <u>inflate</u> the raft.

    • fill with air   • float   • lift

3. At last the great clouds began to <u>wane</u>.

    • turn white   • get smaller   • move faster

2 **For each item, find the correct spelling of the word. Then circle it.**

1. clean
   cleen

2. dayntee
   dainty

3. docter
   doctor

4. shoulder
   sholder

END OF TEST 12

Name _____

TEST 13

1 Write the letter of the picture that shows the correct meaning.

1. The <u>bat</u> flew in through the window. ___
2. She <u>clips</u> the bushes every two weeks. ___
3. The <u>bat</u> hit the ball very hard. ___
4. Paper <u>clips</u> don't cost much. ___

A.

B.

C.

D.

Mastery Test 13   T-39

TEST 13

2 Write the words in order from driest to wettest.

1. _____
2. _____
3. _____
4. _____

saturated
damp
soaked
wet

3 Write the words in order from making the biggest pieces to the smallest pieces.

1. _____
2. _____
3. _____
4. _____

dice
chop
grind
slice

END OF TEST 13